# ENGLISH POETRY
## — OF THE —
# FIRST WORLD WAR

George Parfitt has also written:

*Ben Jonson: Private man and public poet*
*English Poetry of the Seventeenth Century*
*John Donne: a literary life*
*English Fiction of the First World War*

and has edited:

*Ben Jonson: The complete poems*
*Silver Poets of the Seventeenth Century*
*The Plays of Cyril Tourneur*
*John Dryden: Selected criticism* (with James Kinsley)
*The Courtship Narrative of Leonard Wheatcroft* (with Ralph Houl-brooke)

# ENGLISH POETRY

## — OF THE —

# FIRST WORLD WAR

## CONTEXTS AND THEMES

## George Parfitt

*Reader in English Literature*
*University of Nottingham*

HARVESTER
WHEATSHEAF

New York • London • Toronto • Sydney • Tokyo • Singapore

First published 1990 by
Harvester Wheatsheaf,
66 Wood Lane End, Hemel Hempstead,
Hertfordshire, HP2 4RG
A division of
Simon & Schuster International Group

Printed and bound in Great Britain by
Billings and Sons Limited, Worcester

Typeset in 10/12pt Plantin
by Witwell Ltd, Southport

British Library Cataloging in Publication Data

Parfitt, George
English poetry of the first world war: contexts and themes.
1. English poetry 20th century History and criticism
I. Title
821.91209

ISBN 0-7108-1285-X
ISBN 0-7108-1286-8 pbk

*For Harold and Ida Bell, with love and gratitude*

# CONTENTS

# PREFACE

This short book is, in a sense, a companion volume to my earlier *English Fiction of the First World War*, both books being attempts to open up their subjects. But the problem was different in the two cases: so far as the fiction is concerned, it has been neglected in favour of the poetry; while the latter has been in danger of death by orthodoxy.

I am well aware that I have said nothing about the vast majority of those who wrote verse during and/or about the First World War, but I have attempted to represent something of its range without getting into counter-productive details. This book is not a history of English poetry of the First World War. It is, rather, a set of essays on aspects of the poetry which call for further examination or reconsideration. So the book is, in a sense, parasitic on earlier studies of the material, while the idea of 'further examination or reconsideration' explains aspects of emphasis or selection.

A chapter has, for instance, been given exclusively to Robert Graves, and this is a departure from the overall structure of the book. This has been done partly because the publication of William Graves's edition of Robert Graves's poems of the war has, in making these poems available again, made a reassessment of Robert Graves's achievement as a poet of the war both more feasible and more necessary. Also, that achievement has been understated. It does not, however, follow that in giving Graves a chapter I am claiming that he is the most important English poet of the war.

It might, quite reasonably, be felt that too much attention has been paid to Ivor Gurney, at the expense of, in particular, Wilfred Owen. But Gurney has been undervalued, while Owen has had a lot of ink spent on him – his poetry is in less need of critical attention. Here again the allocation of space is not, of itself, a value judgement.

There is also the question of David Jones, for whose work large claims are sometimes made, but who is almost entirely ignored here. Such neglect is unjust, if Jones is seen as primarily a poet; and I can only say that I do not see Jones in this way and that I feel unable to write about his work with any authority or conviction.

The effort, then, is to ask questions and to encourage readers to do the same (perhaps by seeking answers in other books). I hope that an attitude to the First World War (and to war at large) is defined in this book. The material demands an attitude and books that purport to be neutral are usually boring. For the record, I am a socialist and a pacifist. My beliefs necessarily condition my responses, and I know that other people hold other beliefs.

Finally, both the books I have written about literature of the First World War owe a great deal to seminars I have had with students at the University of Nottingham: I am grateful for the interest the relevant students have shown. Maureen did not produce the index, having much better things to do, but her love and support have been vital.

George Parfitt

# 1

# OVERVIEWS

## CAUSES AND CONDITIONS OF THE WAR

The immediate cause of the First World War seems simple enough: the assassination of Archduke Ferdinand at Sarajevo (in Yugoslavia) in June 1914. So far as Britain's involvement is concerned, that was virtually ensured by the German violation of Belgian neutrality and formalised by Germany's ignoring of the British ultimatum to withdraw from Belgian soil. A.J.P. Taylor begins *The First World War: An illustrated history* with an account of the marriage between Ferdinand and Countess Sophie Chotek, but within three paragraphs has reached the assassination.[1] Eric Hobsbawm speaks of 'The rest' following 'inexorably' from Germany's decision to give full backing to Austria in the aftermath of the events at Sarajevo.[2]

Such simplicities say little, however, and Hobsbawm reminds us that 'Probably more ink has flowed, more trees have been sacrificed to make paper, more typewriters have been busy, to answer [the question of the origins of the war] than any other in history'.[3] Clearly, there can be little chance of 'explaining' the coming of the war in a brief introduction to a short book about English poetry in the war. The safest generalisations would seem to be that there was no single cause and that, rather than a plurality, it is better to think in terms of a complex of causes. Further, the best advice to give the unwary may be to be suspicious of grand sweeping explanations based on such concepts as 'German character' or 'French taste for revanche'. Various modes of analysis may contribute to fuller understanding – from deep structural socio-political explanations to teleological ones and to those which stress narrative chains and triggers. There are also reductivist presentations which, including everything, exclude all possibility of explanation, leaving us with 'accident', coincidence, fate or God's will. Some accounts concentrate upon the situation of the European powers in the decade before 1914, while others seem to feel that the history of how this war came into being should be a history of the world to that date.

Basil Liddell Hart opens the 1970 version of his history of the war with a chapter on its origins; and he says at one point that 'the fundamental causes of the conflict can be epitomised in three words – fear, hunger, pride'.[4] The problem, of course, is that these three words can explain so much about human behaviour that they offer little specific illumination of any particular event. But Hart's desire to epitomise does, at least, hold him back from indulging the fallacy of the single simple cause, and his chapter offers a succinct survey of contributory factors. He begins by summarising contributions on a nation-by-nation basis, touching on German expansionism, the legacy which made Austro-Hungary an artificial and unstable entity, the fear generated by Russia ('perhaps the deadliest of all the ingredients in the final detonation', p. 17), the mixture of fear and self-confidence in France after 1870, and Britain's 'slow awakening to the reality of Germany's feeling towards her' (ibid.).

Even so brief a survey is valuable in suggesting a spread of causes at the expense of any single cause (British arrogance, German 'barbarism'), but it is, in itself, limited by being synchronic and static. Hart's survey of nations can only contribute to explanation by becoming diachronic and dynamic; and so further complications are inevitable, as, to be fair, Hart implicitly recognises.

There is, for example, the need to consider the internal situation within the relevant nations and how this contributes to and/or cuts across the national attitudes just exemplified. Hart himself points to 'the popular unrest' in Russia and 'the clamour for universal suffrage in Germany' as encouraging what he calls the 'war-parties' in those countries to keep an eye upon war as a possible 'safety-valve' (p.36). What this should hint at is a dialectic within the countries concerned; a complex interaction of forces helping to shape foreign policy through the imperatives of domestic. When Barbara Tuchman refers to the sociological investigations of Rowntree, Booth and Chiozza Money as providing evidence that one-third of Britain's population was living 'in chronic poverty, unable to sustain the primal needs of animal life',[5] she suggests the possibility that, for some of the British privileged, war might help contain the social problem. It is certainly worth recalling that almost 1,000 strikes took place in Britain between January and July 1914; and that the growth of trade unionism (there were more than 4 million trade union members by 1914) might suggest a sharpening edge to class struggle.

If we move from the living conditions of deprived individuals, through the histories and ambitions of the relevant nations, to aspects of internationalism, we add a further dimension, one which is itself plural. The diplomacy of the major powers in the nineteenth and early twentieth centuries created a defence against war which, it can be argued, paradoxically, facilitated conflict in 1914: Germany had commitments to Austro-Hungary, Britain to France. Tuchman quotes the Dutch pastor Domela Nieuwenhuis: 'Let all workers regardless of nationality strike on the declaration of war and there will be no war!' (p. 285), while Hobsbawm reminds us that 'the Labour and Socialist International . . . committed itself in 1907 to an international strike against war' (p. 325). Hobsbawm argues that politicians were not seriously bothered by such phenomena (and, of course, the type of collectivist call envisaged failed miserably in 1914), but it may be that class-based fears about such proletarian internationalism helped create a climate for war. So Hobsbawm sees such things as the institution of the Nobel Peace Prize (1897) and the first Hague Peace Conference (1899) as international manifestations of fear of war.

There is also, of course, the economic factor. By some accounts (most famously, Normal Angell's *The Great Illusion* of 1910) economic forces had reached such a stage of international interdependence that war could not happen or, if it did, would collapse within a few months. (The reality was very different, with economic internationalism having 'a good war'.) But, for others, economic competition is seen as a major factor in encouraging war. So Hobsbawm speaks of the 'characteristic' limitlessness of 'capitalist accumulation' as destablising 'the structures of traditional world politics' (p. 318). Zara Steiner notes that 'In 1890 Britain had more registered tonnage than all the rest of the world together' and that in 1903 Chamberlain 'highlighted the question of the German economic threat to the Empire'.[6] As an economic power Britain was, in 1914, still impressive, but the growing challenge to this power from such countries as Germany and the United States created both envy and defensiveness at the international level. Steiner's chapter on 'Britain and Germany' is riddled with evidence of mutual fear and distrust.

It is implausible to expect, beyond these multiples, a single explanation for the coming of the war, but it is dangerous to conclude from this that because the war happened it was inevitable. It is also dangerous to ascribe the war to fate, accident, or God's will, or to claim that all the possible contributory factors were necessary conditions of war. History suggests that the human race is adept at finding occasions for conflict. Marxists and Christians might at least agree that a radical change/revolution is the only way to alter this.

## THE NATURE OF THE WAR

Because of the war of 1939-45, what used to be called the Great War is now more commonly referred to as the First World War. The phrase is perhaps unwarrantably Eurocentric (and a former colleague tells me that a highly-educated Chinese teacher he spoke to recently had scarcely heard of the 1914-18 conflict) but even revisionist writers like John Terraine would hardly deny that 'the Great War' is an appropriate title. Despite the global nature of naval operations,[7] the war was essentially, in terms of location, a European conflict - including the often more-or-less static Western Front - which came to stretch from Switzerland to the Channel; the more volatile Eastern Front, which at one time reached deep into Russia; and the eastern European theatre most famous for the Gallipoli landings. There were operations elsewhere (notably on the African continent) but the focus was always on Europe.

A list of the nations involved in the war, however, makes the claim that this was a world war more plausible, especially when the United States joined the allies in April 1917. But even before that, the existence and involvement of the British Empire ensured world-wide participation. The presence of 'White Commonwealth' troops is well known and has generated its own history, literature and myth; but Africa, the Indian sub-continent, and smaller units of the Empire were also represented, by troops and in support. What had its immediate origins in an assassination in the obscurity of Sarajevo became a struggle with implications for countries many thousands of miles away, and for people who had never heard of Sarajevo or of Franz Ferdinand. But if the war is seen as a conflict about dominion in the world, this diffusion becomes understandable; and the territory actually being fought on becomes a synecdoche for the globe. Britain, for instance, had no territorial claims to fight for on the European mainland – but German victory would certainly have had implications for British colonies.

Even in terms of the sites of conflict this was a great war. There had been earlier European wars which had ranged over much of the continent and had afflicted many people (most recently, the Napoleonic Wars), but these had been basically wars of set-piece battles and sieges, involving mainly professional armies which, while large, were modest by the standard of 1914–18. The First World War drew in far more people than any European predecessor, and in a new variety of ways. Combatants have to be measured in millions rather than in thousands or even hundreds of thousands, and millions of combatants mean that millions of families are threatened. Providing for such vast armies means millions in support: non-combatants nursing the wounded, making munitions and other war materials, filling the jobs left vacant by the members of the armed forces who were not professionals. Then there are the effects which followed from the size of the sites of conflict: the refugees, the civilian casualties, the wrecked homes and lands.

It was also, of course, a great war for casualties. It is itself a horror of the war that precise figures are unascertainable. The idea of the 'unknown soldier' extends beyond the concepts of individual ano-nymity to an anonymity of scale. The figures I use are taken from John Terraine's *The Smoke and the Fire*[8] – Terraine being an historian who is anxious to minimise rather than maximise the impact of casualties. Terraine seems to accept that upwards of 9 million were killed and some 20 million wounded. These are combatant figures and they appear to exclude those who were psychologically damaged. Terraine provides tables which measure casualties in other ways: losses of approximately 280,000 by the Austro-Hungarian army in a single week in June 1916, for example, or of some 6,000 daily by the British during the German offensive in Picardy in Spring 1918. Finally, the casualties as a percentage of forces mobilised are striking: 35.8 per cent for the British Empire (including a very small element for prisoners); 64.9 per cent for Germany (1.2 million of the relevant 7.2 million being prisoners); 76.3 per cent for Russia (2.5 million prisoners of 9.1 million).

Terraine has important points to make about British losses as compared with those of other nationalities, about rates of loss as compared with other wars, and about the offensive : defensive ratio.

This is all in the cause of demystifying aspects of the war (and of renovating Haig's reputation). But Terraine can do nothing (because there is nothing to be done) to remove the awfulness of the facts, an awfulness which the statistics can only gesture towards. The rest – the degradation of bodies and devastation of psyches – cannot be counted. And, remembering our subject – English poetry of the war – it should be added that combatants, at least, were always aware of the casualties at the immediate level, and had to find ways of living with such awareness.

Our images of war tend to be army ones, and the First World War was not one of great naval battles, even though naval competition between Britain and Germany was a contributory factor to the outbreak of the war. This was a matter both of competition in building more powerful fighting ships (now able to shell at ranges measured in miles) and at the mercantile level. The naval dimension of the war is not so much a matter of major battles at sea (there being only one of these – the inconclusive affair at Jutland) but is to be seen in the cross-referencing of military and mercantile in the economic-naval blockade of Germany, the German submarine attack on Allied shipping (which nearly starved the British Isles to defeat), and the German attack on the *Lusitania*, which did so much to bring the United States into the war.

The creation of better warships and the development of the submarine and torpedo were matched by technological refinements in the air and on land. Tracing the references to operations in the air in the index to Hart's *History* back into his text gives a sense of how air warfare was transformed between 1914 and 1918. By the end of the war, Britain had a Royal Air Force and some limited experience of being attacked from the sky. Meanwhile, and remembering that air-operations had a direct bearing on land warfare, the technology of armies was also transformed. Famously, 1914–18 saw the coming of the tank (if rather hesitantly), the use of gas (although its impact was as much psychological as physical), major developments with machine guns, effective long-range shelling and large-scale military mining. Simultaneously, there was the growing obsolescence of the sword, the horse and the pitched battle. Most notable, perhaps, were developments in shells and trenches, the two being interconnected.

Perhaps the greatest cliché image of the war is of the trenches and the troops in them; and it is perhaps the case that the trench stasis has been exaggerated, for men were frequently on the move, even if much of this movement was into front-line trenches, from reserve or rest or hospital, perhaps leave, out of them into raid or attack, or along the trench network. There were also passages of fluid warfare. Yet it remains true that the strip on the Western Front which was fought over was, for long periods, both narrow and static, relative to the forces involved and the significance of the conflict. Moreover, the sophistication of trench-lines prompted developments in the power and quality of weapons, which, in reaction, prompted further defensive sophistication. A recurrent feature of the record of experience in the Front Line is the effort to pin down the aural, visual and psychological impact of shelling. This constituted a long-range assault which the individual soldier in the trenches could neither respond to directly nor confidently avoid.

Finally, in this section, it is important to touch on aspects of the war at home. The British were, in a direct sense, sheltered; Zeppelin raids and civilian casualties are almost invisible when compared to the civilian experience in the Second World War or to the First World War experience of civilians in Russia, Germany, France or Belgium. But the shock to ideas of British invulnerability should be noted (even though invasion scares were hardly new). Other developments were, however, more striking from a British viewpoint. The mobilisation of mass armies created greater opportunities for women in the job-market and, although many of these work-gains scarcely survived the end of the war, the socio-sexual effects were important. Above all, the scale and duration of the war were such as to mark almost everyone and every aspect of British life at home. Edward Thomas, famously, wrote, in 'As the Team's Head Brass' of a fallen elm which , the poem's ploughman says, will only be moved 'when the war's over'. It is a detail which can act as a symbol of how far the war reached out. How durable that reaching was is perhaps best rendered as the silence of those who still repress their memories.

## THE CLIMATE FOR POETS IN 1914

To many combatants the First World War seemed phenomenal, and the problem how to communicate any sense of it to 'outsiders' is a recurrent theme. This problem – the grim novelty of the war – was exacerbated by a number of factors. Many combatants lacked (as we shall see) the skills to communicate anything very much on paper, while many were inhibited by the decent desire not to distress those at home with unpleasant details. Moreover, there was, at times, the feeling that Home was not very interested in the war, and/or that the ubiquity of disinformation discouraged truth-telling.

Poets are expected to be more than competent in expressing themselves, for their business is words. But we have become increasingly aware since Saussure of how untrustworthy words are, of the gaps between signifier and signified, of elusiveness, allusiveness and multi-referentiality. Words have histories and subjectivities; are tainted and value-laden. Poets who tried to make words speak truth of the war had no chance of evading such features of the medium they were using; and it should be added that there is a 'politics' of verse form. To write a sonnet or use heroic couplets cannot be an innocent act. Finally, in this context we are not talking only, or primarily, about consciousness: a writer participates in such linguistic and formal characteristics of her/his medium whether she/he wants to do so or not.

It is widely known that the declaration of war was greeted with mass enthusiasm and expression of patriotic fervour. This was not the case only in Britain. Peter Gay speaks of 'a war psychosis', whereby 'the war seemed a release from boredom, an invitation to heroism, a remedy for decadence', adding that 'it was in Germany that this psychosis reached heights of absurdity'.[9] In Britain there was a well-established style for 'public' verse which was appropriate for the prevalent sentiments felt at the outbreak of war, and which might have served for the type of war which many thought this would be. This style can even be seen as a preparation for war; and it is well exemplified in W.E. Henley's 'A New Song to an Old Tune', which begins:

> Sons of Shannon, Tamar, Trent,
> Men of the Lothians, men of Kent,
> Essex, Wessex, shore and shire,
> Mates of the net, the mine, the fire,
> Lads of desk and wheel and loom,
> Noble and trader, squire and groom,
> Come where the bugles of England play,
> *Over the hills and far away!*

This, from the volume *For England's Sake* (1900), which is significantly sub-titled 'Verses and songs in time of war', is rhythmically regular and verbally undemanding, using alliteration, internal rhyme and proper names to create a sense of national unity. The place names suggest (especially as underlined by alliteration and rhyme) that the British Isles make up a coherent whole, subsumed to the concept 'England'. There is also faint anachronism, an exclusively male stress and a blithe obliteration of tensions between classes and occupations. Henley does not so much ignore industrialisation as render it harmless, distancing its actuality by generalisation and anachronism. The drive is to establish, by way of the creation of unity, the idea that no sacrifice is too great for 'the One Flag', and 'the One Race':

What if the best of our wages be
An empty sleeve, a stiff-set knee,
A crutch for the rest of life – who cares,
So long as the One Flag floats and dares?

This is a non-analytic style which depends heavily upon incantation and icon (Flag, Race), explicitly articulating values and beliefs which serve and shape the desired 'national' aim – the commitment to defence through militarism. It is not too much to say that such writing exploits the shiftiness of words mentioned earlier, and it does this partly by suppressing whatever might call into question the values and beliefs being endorsed. Henley's lines, by marginalising and suppressing that which might subvert the endorsed account, provide a classic example of how dominant ideology uses subversions to justify its suppressions. As such, his poem is an instance of what some poets of the First World War were to struggle to deconstruct.

There are variants on this manner. Henry Newbolt concentrates upon invoking a glorious version of military history –

*Oh! to see the linstock lighting,*
   *And to hear the round shot biting,*
*For we're all in love with fighting*
   *On the Fighting Temeraire.*

                                                    *('The Fighting Temeraire')*

– and on fusing the idea of the fellowship of the so-called public schools with that of life as battle:

To-day and here the fight's begun,
   Of the great fellowship you're free;
Henceforth the School and you are one,

And what You are, the race shall be.

('Clifton Chapel')[10]

Newbolt's 'history' glosses over the fact that the tradition he is invoking is a relatively new invention (Clifton, for example, was only 'reconstituted' as a public school in 1862), while the arrogance of defining the 'race' in this way is both impertinent and, decoded, a version of the real power of the privileged to dictate the national ethos. But it is William Watson who shows most clearly how the style in question can disarm subversion through blandness:

Too long the gulf betwixt
This man and that fixt
    Yawns yet unspanned.
Too long, that some may rest,
Tired millions toil unblest,
God lift our lowliest,
    God save this land!

('A New National Anthem')[11]

This is superficially unexceptionable, in that it recognises inequality and purports to oppose it. But the writing betrays its own sentiments, in that its inadequacy overthrows optimism. The image of the gulf is symptomatic, being so tired as a figure of division that, 'Yawn' as it may, it cannot, without drastic renovation, do anything towards amelioration. Moreover, shifting the onus of change onto God is an old trick the powerful play, and always evades the realities of social history.

It should be added that, before 1914, Rudyard Kipling had shown that the confident and regular rhythms of such verse could be made to serve quite subtle, even radical ends, but it remains true that this nationalistic public style was hardly usable in the circumstances of the Great War, a war which mocked chivalry and chauvinism alike. This, however, did not stop some poets of the war from trying to sustain the manner of Newbolt and Watson.

A confident sense of national identity and superiority, and a matching confidence in the merits of rousing rhythms and comfortably 'poetic' language, mark this poetry, but they also cut it off from what is most interesting in the practice of the – usually younger – writers known as the Georgians. These poets, in the years immediately before the war, were consciously seeking alternatives to Newbolt and his kind. In the volume *Georgian Poetry 1913–1915*, which Edward Marsh published in November 1915, there is work by a number of poets who are known in part for their attempts to write

about the war: Brooke, Gibson, Hodgson and Ledwidge. The titles
of the poems Marsh prints suggest, by the standards of Watson and
Newbolt, considerable modesty of objective: 'The Bull' (Hodgson),
'Milk for the Cat' (Monro), 'A Town Window' (Drinkwater). These
poets are more inclined to attempt the 'sordid' or 'humble' topic
(although Henley had a line in this). So Davies writes about a
prostitute:

> Here comes Kate Summers, who, for gold,
>   Takes any man to bed
>
> ('The Bird of Paradise')

And de la Mare about farmers:

> Three jolly Farmers
> Once bet a pound
> Each dance the others would
> Off the ground. . . .
>
> ('Off the Ground')

The Georgians are interested in myth and legend (Flecker, 'The
Old Ships') and in faery (especially de la Mare), but they are not
greatly concerned with the nation or the national past, at least as
defined by Newbolt. They tend to be technically conservative, rather
than innovatory, but meditation rather than incantation is characteristic:

> All day they loitered by the resting ships,
> Telling their beauties over, taking stock;
> At night the verdict left my messmates' lips,
> 'The *Wanderer* is the finest ship in dock'.
>
> (Masefield, 'The *Wanderer*')

This is reminiscent of the Tennyson of 'Ulysses' rather than that of
'The Charge of the Light Brigade', the latter being a source for the
style of such as Newbolt.

Yet, although the Georgians prided themselves on their realism, it
is not easy to claim that the dominant Georgian manner constituted a
style which could cope with, or survive, the war. Drinkwater begins
a brief lyric with these lines:

> Beyond my window in the night
>   Is but a drab inglorious street,
> Yet there the frost and clean starlight
>   As over Warwick woods are sweet.
>
> ('A Town Window')

The war was to insist that its 'drab inglorious' streets be confronted more precisely than here, or transformed into less agreeable phenomena than 'frost and clean starlight'. At their best, the Georgians show the desire the respond to the actuality of the early twentieth century without the capacity to render this adequately in verse. There is an ubiquitous tendency to slide off in the direction of the pretty. It might also be suggested that the Georgian achievement would prove of most use to poets of the war as articulating a vision of what no longer was. It then becomes a kind of parody, along the lines of what Siegfried Sassoon was to do in prose with the *Memoirs of George Sherston*. The only Georgian who found a satisfactory way of modulating Georgian style to war experience was, it will be argued later, W.W. Gibson.

A glance back from 1914 at what poetry had been published in Britain since the turn of the century indicates the strength of the styles so far discussed. Henley's *For England's Sake* was published in 1900 and his *Works* in 1908; Watson's *For England* came out in 1903, Newbolt's *Songs of the Fleet* in 1910 and his *Poems Old and New* in 1912 – the latter also being the starting point for the first Georgian poetry volume. By 1912, some of Marsh's Georgians, moreover, had been publishing volumes for several years: de la Mare's *Songs of Childhood* came out in 1902, as did Masefield's *Salt Water Ballads*, while Lascelles Abercrombie's *Interludes and Poems* appeared in 1908.

There were alternatives to the styles mentioned above. Thomas Hardy's lyric manner recognised the grimness in experience which the war would emphasise, while *The Dynasts* can be seen as prophetic of the war itself. But Hardy was to write some awful war poetry and his finest verse seems to have made little impact on the poets with whom we are concerned. W. B. Yeats was both established and experienced by 1914, but it is only with *Responsibilities* of that year that he finds his major voice. More intriguingly, Pound (*Personae*, 1909; *Ripostes*, 1912) acts as a reminder that Modernism precedes the war and was both to influence and be influenced by it – but I know of no English poet of the war who used Modernist techniques and perspectives from its beginning. Another way of putting this would be to say that expectations of the war were anti-Modernist and that it took experience of what the war was actually like to indicate Modernism's relevance to it. Finally, one might notice the developing interest, by 1914, in seventeenth-century metaphysical poetry and in Jacobean drama. Brooke, for instance, was influenced by such writing before the war, but his few war poems look elsewhere – again, perhaps, because of what the war was expected to be like.

## WAR POETRY AND THE WAR POETS

There is a stereotype here: for many people, a poet of the First World War is a handsome young officer who writes either about country and heroism (Rupert Brooke) or about the horrors of trench and bombardment (Wilfred Owen, Siegfried Sassoon). For rather fewer people this image may be replaced or overlaid by the more disturbing pictures of Ivor Gurney or Isaac Rosenberg, but it is the Brooke/Sassoon stereotype which has been dominant; and it is one which was manufactured within the period of the war itself, as is clear, for example, in A. St John Adcock's memorial volume *For Remembrance*.[12] Its frontispiece is Sherril Schell's photograph of Brooke, while text and illustrations work to present a sense of selfless, heroic, largely patrician British manhood. Adcock's sub-title is 'Soldier poets who have fallen in the war', and the young men he memorialises are to be seen as the flower of a generation being destroyed to save the nation.[13] The book is an obvious example of hagiography, although it is only fair to add that the obverse to this, which emphasises the horrors and degradation of war, as seen, for example, in the break-up of Gurney, the pathetic details of bewildered rankers shot for cowardice[14] and the mutiny at Etaples, have been seen by some as a manipulation of the evidence. This has emerged most recently with the objections to the television version of *The Monocled Mutineer*.[15]

For most people who know anything about the war in English poetry, there is a shortlist of the 'best' poets of that war which consists simply of Owen and Sassoon. A slightly longer version would perhaps bring in Brooke, Rosenberg, Edmund Blunden, Edward Thomas, Ivor Gurney and Charles Sorley. These eight have in common that they were all combatants who saw action (although in Brooke's case very little). Five of them were killed (Owen, Brooke, Rosenberg, Thomas and Sorley), while a sixth (Gurney) spent most of his post-war life in mental hospitals. All were male; all but Rosenberg and Gurney were officers; all were young. Thomas, in his mid-thirties in 1914, is a partial exception to this last point, but he is the only member of this group who was over 30 at the start of the war. Blunden was 18; Sorley a year older.

A breakdown of some 200 poets of the war produces a rather sharper profile of a 'typical' English war poet: a young Army subaltern, educated at a fee-paying school and Oxford or Cambridge, whose social standing is professional/genteel. My sample is incomplete, in that in a number of cases full information is lacking, but it is, I think, representative enough. According to my information, only some 12 per cent of the sample went to state schools and, of the poets known to have entered higher education, 75 per cent went to Oxford or Cambridge. So far as I can see, only about one in twenty of these poets could be called plebeian. The vast majority of them served in the Army, and some 60 per cent were subalterns, most of these (as we should expect) being under 30 in 1914. R.E. Vernede (39 at the start of the war) marks the upward limit; Edgell Rickword (16/17) the downward.

Such information underpins the stereotype, and it is important to keep this picture in mind, since it inevitably influences the overall view of the war as represented in the poetry. The war, as seen by young officers of privileged background, is likely to be a picture defined by the social shaping of such men. Julian Grenfell's war was never likely to be Isaac Rosenberg's. But it should be added that this stereotype is also a distortion in another sense, for, while it clearly has validity (these patrician males did serve and observe), it marginalises other significant groups, groups which, differing within themselves, may offer variant views of the war. Even where such groups are very small we should remember that, at lest potentially, they might see the war in ways which represent alternatives to the stereotype.

Within the Army, the prominence of subalterns among the war poets is, obviously enough, at the expense of rankers, NCOs and Staff officers. The subaltern shared the rigours of front-line experience with NCOs and rankers, but his experience could hardly be the same: he had privileges and he had the specific responsibilities of his rank. Moreover, his perceptions of experience would also be different, since he had a different social context. The subaltern would be likely to have strong social links with the Staff, although this would be qualified by age differences (at least *vis-à-vis* senior Staff officers) and by the fact that Staff was dominated by professional soldiers while most subalterns, as the war developed, were non-professionals. The subaltern also, most importantly, lived in the context of the Front Line and can, in fact, be seen as a vital link in the Army hierarchy: physically in close contact with men of very different backgrounds to his own, while socio-culturally close to Staff. For reasons to be discussed later, there is relatively little surviving ranker poetry, while Staff verse is also at a premium.

Forces poetry is dominated by the Army. I know of about twelve Army poets for every Navy poet and nineteen for every flier poet. This is partly a reflection of the sheer size which the Army reached during the war and partly a matter of where dominant interest in the war lay and lies. It may also have something to do with environment (a man in the trenches had more opportunity to write than a pilot), but the important point is simply that naval and aerial responses are under-represented. It is, though, perhaps more important to stress that much of the war's poetry was produced from beyond the stereotype.

Until Virago published Catherine Reilly's anthology, *Scars upon my Heart* in 1981, for example, modern readers might well have been almost totally unaware that women wrote poetry about the war. Gardner (1964), Black (1970) and Silkin (1979) all produced anthologies of poetry of the war without a single poem by a woman. Hussey (1967) included one such poem (by Alice Meynell) and Parsons (1965) chose one each by Charlotte Mew and Fredegond Shove. It may perhaps be an indication of the impact of Reilly's anthology that Hibberd and Onions's (1986) has twelve women poets (out of 100) and that such poets are treated at length by Nosheen Khan[16]. It is, though, salutary to recall that as long ago as 1923, Jacqueline Trotter included twenty-one poems by women in a collection of 144.[17] A number of the women who wrote poems about the war had experience of it as auxiliaries, while others had the loss of husbands, lovers, sons or brothers to cope with. Women experienced the war in a number of ways, and to ignore or marginalise their war is a distortion of the complete record.

Among male poets of the war, moreover, there were many civilians, and a reader of such novels as *The Pretty Lady* and *Lord Raingo* (both by Arnold Bennett) or of H.G. Wells's *Mr Britling Sees it Through* should be aware of some of the ways in which civilian experience complements, rather than duplicates, military. Some of these male civilians were senior and well-established writers by 1914, men who had already had a lot of experience and might be expected to have strong preconceptions about the war. William Watson was 56 in 1914; Sir Arthur Conan Doyle had served in the Boer War and been knighted in 1902; John Galsworthy (47 in 1914) was famous as a novelist *(Man of Property*, 1903) and playwright *(Strife*, 1909); while Rudyard Kipling, almost 50 in 1914, had been a popular writer of stories and verse since the 1890s. Hardy was a famous novelist; Yeats an experienced poet; Housman's *A Shropshire Lad* had come out as early as 1896; Bridges was Poet Laureate. Henry Newbolt was 46, Hardy well past 70. They do not form a group, and their production of war poetry varies considerably in quantity and manner, but they do represent a significant body of response.

This senior body of civilian writers was, by 1914, under pressure from a younger generation, many of whom, as we should expect, served in the war. But there are several who did not and who deviate interestingly from the social profile of the stereotype: G.K. Chesterton went from St Paul's to the Slade to train as an artist; John Drinkwater had his higher education at the University of Birmingham; D.H. Lawrence, child of a mining family, went to train as a teacher at Nottingham University (College). Walter de la Mare and Drinkwater worked as clerks (the latter also as an actor), while Lawrence was briefly a teacher in a state school. Potentially, such men might write of the war to very different effect from a Brooke or a Sassoon.

'Potentially' is, however, an important word, for there were pressures which encouraged poets who wrote of the war to conform to expectations. Sassoon experienced censorship, and it may well be that, towards the war's end, the pressures to write from the perspectives of disillusionment were considerable.[18] Yet it is important to remember this potential for difference, for there is much more work to be done before we can be clear how much or how little of it there is between the various categories of poets. Our thinking about English poetry should, in the meanwhile, be based on an awareness of how narrow the stereotype focus is. This focus has it that the poetic truth of the war is the perspective of the young male subaltern in the trenches of the Western Front: one war among many.

It is thus worth looking a little more closely at what English poetry of the war can be expected to be, or, more precisely, at what its emphases are. In so far as such poetry can be thought of as a corpus,

it is overwhelmingly dominated by the short lyric. The poems reflect
the foci of British experience and interest – on the Western Front
above all, with a secondary concern with the Balkans. The Eastern
Front is largely ignored. This leads to the obvious, but important,
point that English poetry of the war is centred upon the native
experience; so that any effort to consider how poetry at large treated
the war should properly be a multi-lingual enterprise.[19] Given this
orientation, there are two main concentrations in the relevant poetry.
The first of these is again obvious enough: the attention given to the
ideas and actuality of fighting, whether the writer was a combatant
or not. This concentration, as will be shown later, involves both
attempts at reportage and conscious or unconscious mediations
between the conditions of fighting in the war and expectations based
on earlier warfare and writings about that. The second main
emphasis is on Home experience of the war, wherein Home is
usually seen as the recipient of Front experience. The defining factor
is awareness of the Front and of conditions there (whether accurately
known or distorted by varieties of propaganda and suppression). The
poetry of the war seldom considers either Staff perspectives (except
satirically) or those of government. Political analysis is rare,
represented either by invocations of national will or by assaults upon
government as concerned only to promote slaughter. The concentration upon fighting may be expressed from the perspective of the
officer (usually a subaltern) or, more rarely, of the ranker, but we
shall also see that there is a marked tendency to proceed on the basis
that these perspectives are essentially the same. Such concentration
ranges from stress upon the individual, through the expression of
group mentality (usually at the level of the squad rather than the
regiment or division), to the attempted representation of the soldier
as some sort of Everyman.

    As the previous paragraph may suggest, there are large areas of
what goes to make up the First World War which English poetry of
the war largely ignores. Taking 'English poetry of the war' to mean
here poetry in English by residents in the British Isles, we have a
body of work which rarely concerns itself with responses of the non-
British. There are partial exceptions – poems which attempt a
German perspective; a few which represent French, Belgian, American or Colonial viewpoints – but there are not many of these. The
poetry we are considering has little to say of the causes of the war,
except for some blanket condemnation of the enemy (whether this be

the Germans or 'traitors' at home), and little to say about the sequence of events in the war. The stress is upon incidents and conditions, rather than upon campaigns and battles, although it should be added that this stress is itself revealing, both of the limited viewpoint possible for subalterns and rankers and of the tendency of this war to be inchoate, hard to define or discuss in the traditional terms of battles and campaigns. From this it follows that there is little to be said of strategy or tactics. The dominant concern with trench experience and small groups leads to a focusing upon the giving and receiving of orders and upon experiences which are immediate and which largely obliterate any interest in wider issues of planning. Such responses as there are to the latter tend to be resigned or sardonic. The thinking and planning of Staff and Home are present in the poetry of the war chiefly – where represented at all – as objects of resentment.

Two further points should be made about what aspects of the war are represented or understressed. The first is that, although there is a considerable body of verse which enacts Home perspectives, there is relatively little account or analysis of socio-economic conditions. The effects of the war on Home are (understandably enough) largely seen in terms of the emotional cost. The second point concerns the idea of the enemy, and all that needs to be said here is that, while the poetry has a strong sense of enemies as forces inimical to the survival or welfare of the individual or group, it does not express a powerful sense of the notional enemy. There is, of course, poetry which is explicitly directed at the enemy – the kind of anathematising which we shall see in Bertram Dobell – but such writing comes to be dominated by poetry which sees the notional enemy as either essentially the same as the writer or her/his persona, or which ignores this enemy in favour of concentrating upon other aspects of war experience. And, as just suggested, there is the poetry which relocates the idea of the enemy, whereby (as most famously with Sassoon) the true enemy is Home or at home.

The main chapters of this book seek to take into account the factors and caveats of the last two sections of this introduction. They cannot pretend to constitute a 'history' of English poetry of the war. They are perhaps better seen as essays in the cause of opening up a subject which has been in danger of being closed down into a comfortable orthodoxy.

## NOTES

1. Hamish Hamilton, 1963.
2. *The Age of Empire*, Book Club Associates, 1987, p. 323.
3. ibid., p. 309.
4. *History of the First World War* (1970), Book Club Associates, 1975, p. 18.
5. *The Proud Tower* (1962), Macmillan, 1980, p. 356.
6. *Britain and the Origins of the First World War*, Macmillan, 1977, pp. 13, 15.
7. See A.A. Hoehling, *The Great War at Sea*, Barker, n.d.
8. (1980), Book Club Associates, 1981.
9. *Weimar Culture* (1969), Penguin, 1988, p. 12.
10. *Collected Poems*, Nelson, n.d., pp. 19, 130.
11. *Collected Poems*, John Lane, 1898, p. 206.
12. Hodder and Stoughton, n.d.
13. On this theme see Robert Wohl, *The Generation of 1914*, Weidenfeld and Nicolson, 1980.
14. See Anthony Babington, *For the Sake of Example*, Leo Cooper, 1983.
15. William Allison and John Fairley, *The Monocled Mutineer*, Quartet, 1979.
16. *Women's Poetry of the First World War*, Harvester Wheatsheaf, 1988.
17. *Valour and Vision* (1920), Hopkinson, new/enlarged edition, 1923.
18. See Sassoon's own notes in *The War Poems*, Faber, 1983.
19. E.A. Marsland's MS., 'First World War Poetry and the Nation's Cause', to be published (I hope) by Routledge and Kegan Paul, goes some way to supply the need.

# 2

# CLEANSING AND RUPERT BROOKE

Rupert Brooke was 27 years old when the First World War began, and his reputation as a poet of that war depends almost entirely on the five 'War Sonnets' published in *New Numbers* in 1915. These poems, together with 'Grantchester', are the central texts of a Brooke legend which also derives from Edward Marsh's hagiographic memoir of 1915, Sherril Schell's photograph of 1913 and the timing and setting of Brooke's death and burial. Brooke died on St George's Day 1915 (of blood-poisoning) on his way to Gallipoli, and was buried on the Greek island of Skyros.

Brooke was of a privileged background. His father was a master at Rugby and he was educated there and at King's College, Cambridge, where he was a founder of the Marlowe Society and a Fabian. He spent 1913 travelling in Canada, the United States and the Pacific, apparently to recover from a nervous breakdown. Earlier he had visited continental Europe. By 1914 he was a known poet, whose first volume had been published in 1911, and a friend of such as John Masefield, Lascelles Abercrombie and John Drinkwater.

To read the poems written before the war is to have a mixed experience, and perhaps to feel that Brooke was something of a slow developer.[1] An early sonnet like 'Success' (January 1910) suggests an ability to think in verse and with verse forms, while there are recurrent indications of interest in idiom and verbal directness, a sense of humour, and – in 'The Old Vicarage, Grantchester' (1912) – a poise which makes that poem a model of patriotic poetry. It is a pity that the fame of the ending –

> yet
> Stands the Church clock at ten to three?
> And is there honey still for tea?

– has blurred awareness of the poem's cool ironies and feeling for detail. But against such qualities must be set Brooke's pursuit of high-sounding banality:

> The inenarrable godhead of delight
>
> ('The Great Lover', 1914)

or

> 'We shall go down with reluctant tread
> "Rose-crowned" into the darkness!'
>
> ('The Hill', 1910)

There is also adolescent unease, particularly about sex:

> fussy *Joy*,
> Who had to catch a train, and *Lust*, poor snivelling boy.
>
> ('The Funeral of Youth', 1913)

or

> her limbs
> That had served Love so well,
> Dust, and a filthy smell.
>
> ('Dead Men's Love', 1911)

Brooke, it should be remembered, was well into his twenties when such lines were written.

Timothy Rogers has remarked that the 'War Sonnets' were 'poems, not of war, but of preparation for war'.[2] One of them in particular, 'The Soldier', quoted in St Paul's by Dean Inge on Easter Sunday 1915 and in *The Times* for 5 April, can be seen as an important document of national preparation for war. Brooke himself was still adjusting to war when he died (having seen action only briefly at Antwerp in 1914), while at his death the nation was still only partially aware of the dimensions of the struggle it had entered. These sonnets have a part to play in such preparation in their construction of an ideology of war which is drawn from pre-war ideologies. This, for Brooke's poetry, includes the simplification of the best of his earlier writings. So sonnet form (by tradition prestigious and mainstream) is used conventionally, humour vanishes, and so does specific detail. The poet's voice is solemn and sonorous.

The 'peace' of the title of the first of these sonnets is primarily that of 'the laughing heart's long peace' (l. 12) which the war is said to have brought about (although it should be noticed that the war is not directly mentioned), but it could also refer to the long years of peace before 1914, years seen as having made 'a world grown old and cold and weary'. What these adjectives implicitly call for is their opposites – youth, warmth and restedness – and it is this call which has been answered by God and the poet in the wakening, the 'clear eye' and sharpened powers of the opening. The transformation is summed up by the image of 'swimmers into cleanness leaping'. This is clearly a tonic experience, reminiscent of the cold water baths of public schools and of the diary of the nineteenth-century priest, Thomas Kilvert, a collocation which links education, muscular Christianity, sexual restraint and moral chastity. Brooke completes his octet by developing his theme of a tired and ageing world, one in which 'sick hearts' cannot be moved by honour, a world of

> half-men, and their dirty songs and dreary,
> And all the little emptiness of love!

What is cleansed here is the sickness of dishonour, effeminacy and love, and such sickness is treated in a suggestive sequence.[3] War makes Man; love is associated with dirt and semi-emasculation. So pre-war is unmanly, a state of adolescent guilt about sex: 'and *Lust*, poor snivelling boy'. There is something here of Keats's 'To a Nightingale', except that Brooke substitutes war for the world of the nightingale. Keats, moreover, brings his poet-figure back from narcosis, while Brooke devotes his sestet to deprecating body, breath, agony and death. This effort marks the poem as propaganda for war: the grim realities are made bland and the word 'war' itself is excluded. Cleanliness was rarely possible for the soldier at the Front in the First World War. Physically, it could become a desired objective; psychologically, Brooke's formulation provided the possibility of feeling morally pure despite physical degradation, and this was part both of the effect of the Brooke myth and of the poems which are part of this myth.

The other sonnets continue the effort at cleansing, an effort which works at several levels. 'Safety' associates security and rest with the safety of immortality ('we have built a house that's not for Time's throwing'), and this is achieved by redefining the word:

> Safe though all safety's lost; safe where men fall;
> And if these poor limbs die, safest of all.

But redefining the word calls for distancing the thing. Brooke could know little of the conditions of this war, which makes the pallor of 'if these poor limbs die, safest of all' hopelessly inadequate. Yet it appears that the poet has either never responded, before the war, to the beauty and grotesquerie of human bodies, or is suppressing his memories in the cause of a positive ideology of war. Brooke's lack of war experience is a fact, but one of limited relevance. What is more to the point is the inadequacy of the response of these poems to experience at large. Paul Delany has reminded us that when Brooke, before the war, worked for the Fabians, he opted to cycle round the countryside of the Home Counties, rather than investigate the heartlands of industrial England.[4]

There is the same cleansing of the physicality of concepts in the first of the two sonnets called 'The Dead' ('Blow Out, You Bugles'). The idea that the dead give the living 'rarer gifts than gold' (l. 3) is a traditional cliché of the privileged, which is given a slight extra edge by 'poor' in the second line. But the ease of the writing degrades what poverty means for the poor, and this degradation prepares the reader for the rewriting of youth as 'red/Sweet wine' which is to be poured out like water; for the glib association of 'work and joy'; for the slick silliness of age as 'unhoped serene'; and for the facile giving up of paternity. (This last can be placed by looking at Ben Jonson's 'On my First Son'). Such factors, so smoothed off, can be summed up as 'dearth' (l. 9) and marginalised to provide space for holiness, love, pain (cleansed by the other two words), honour and nobleness. But since the octet lacks substance, so must the sestet: it is a play of shadows. 'The Dead' is a shimmer of words ('a white/Unbroken glory, a gathered radiance') which abolishes its title and thus serves the national cause, as defined by the national leaders.[5] So 'The Soldier' is the mythical essence of England. His heart, 'all evil shed away', is 'A pulse in the eternal mind' which, giving 'somewhere back the thoughts by England given' makes possible, 'laughter, learnt of friends; and gentleness,/In hearts at peace, under an English heaven'. This peace, however vaguely rendered, is presumably not to be the peace of pre-war, as seen in the first of these sonnets.

The Brooke of the pre-war poems had not been a cleansed figure. He had, it would seem, been troubled by lust and aware of the comic possibilities of a world of fish ('And, sure, the reverent eye must see/ A Purpose in Liquidity' - 'Heaven', 1913), as well as of a grimness beneath Grantchester insouciance:

> (And when they get to feeling old,
> They up and shoot themselves, I'm told).

Everything that checks and troubles in the pre-war poems is cleansed in the 'War Sonnets'; and such cleansing was, it would seem, exactly what the Dean of St Paul's and *The Times* felt the nation needed and wanted. The same humourless sense of conviction runs through Haig's *Private Papers*, with results which were directly destructive.

Some years before 1914, William Watson had prefigured Brooke:

> In Europe live the dregs of Plague to-day,
> Dregs of full many an ancient Plague and dire,
> Old wrongs, old lies of ages blind and cruel.
> What if alone the world-war's world-wide fire
> Can purge the ambushed pestilence away?
>
> ('The World in Armour')[6]

One way of describing how Brooke prepared for the war would be to say that he sought to avoid experience of living by scouring himself with Watson's verse. A moment or two in 'Fragments Written during the Voyage to Gallipoli April 1915' suggest that Brooke might have been beginning to see that the preparation was not enough:

> pity that
> This gay machine of splendour'ld soon be broken,
> Thought little of, pashed, scattered. . . .

Brooke and his cleansing were, as we have seen, promoted by the 'official' nation; and Brooke became the salient factor in a martyrology of the war. It is Schell's photograph which provides the frontispiece for St John Adcock's *For Remembrance*, and Adcock's text offers Brooke as striking a balance between Cavalier and Roundhead traits in the British character; he is thus the ultimate unifier.[7] And when E.B. Osborn, in his similar volume, *The New Elizabethans*, tries to summarise the qualities of the men he writes about, he uses Brookean language, speaking of 'the young heroes of this war like awakening' and of 'that dishonest and dishonourable age' before the war, which now seems 'a sick and meaningless dream'.[8] One of the poems Osborn admires is Julian Grenfell's 'Into Battle', which, according to Osborn, represents war as a 'mode of intense living, harmonious with the deepest nature of man, in which all sham emotions and rootless thoughts and sick sophistries are consumed as in a refiner's fire'.[9] It is characteristic of both Brooke and Osborn that the sonority is all: no facts disturb a reader.

Grenfell was the eldest son of Lord Desborough, educated at Eton and Oxford. He joined the regular army in 1910 and died of wounds received near Ypres in 1915, at almost the same age as Brooke. 'Into Battle' is his only widely-known poem, having been published in *The Times* in 1915 and subsequently in many anthologies. If Osborn's account substitutes myth for history, Grenfell's poem shows how potent myth can be, as he renders battle and death as part of the verities of nature and the seasons:

> The fighting man shall from the sun
>   Take warmth, and life from the glowing earth;
> . . . . . . . . . . . . . . .
> And find, when fighting shall be done,
> Great rest, and fullness after dearth.

The language is Brooke's, and if Brooke's 'Peace' has an uncontrolled slippage from 'half-men' to the 'little emptiness of love', Grenfell's blends some sense of the scale and horror of the war with something nastier. His poem records the 'dreary, doubtful, waiting hours' before action, and the latter is 'brazen frenzy', when 'in the air death moans and sings', but it also presents a 'joy of battle' which 'takes/ [the soldier] by the throat, and makes him blind'. This joy-blind soldier 'shall know,/ Not caring much to know' that life and death are controlled by 'the Destined Will'.[10] The individual is cleansed by becoming a pure and obsessed instrument. What Grenfell describes is, sadly, accurate enough of the experience of some men when fighting, but the irresponsibility of the poem lies in its endorsement of blood-lust as a good and in the slick acceptance of Destined Will. Wars are made on earth by men.

Cleansing can mean any of several cleaning operations, and there is an interesting knot of cleansing images, including ideas of fire, water, awakening and rebirth, which appears in the poems of Laurence Binyon who, in December 1914, published a volume significantly called *The Winnowing Fan: Poems on the Great War*. Binyon, educated at St Paul's and Oxford, began four decades of service in the British Museum in 1893 and, although already in his forties, served as a Red Cross orderly in 1916. The fan of his title purifies grain by separating the wheat from the chaff, and it is this tool which, in 'The Fourth of August', will awaken and purge the earth. The poem marks Britain's entry into the war, and the opening stanza is very close to Brooke's 'Peace'. The 'Spirit of England' ('In the hour of peril purified') is now 'ardent-eyed' and is asked to

'Enkindle this dear earth that bore us'. As this happens, our past cares 'drop out of vision' and 'We step from days of sour division'. Binyon's quatrains (again, as with the sonnet, a comfortingly traditional form) are clear and smooth, enabling phrases like 'the grandeur of our fate' to work subliminally; and, of course, the winnowing fan is itself comfortingly distant from shells, mines and bullets (and reassuringly close to pastoral idylls) so that 'divinely suffering' man in the last line can recall Christ with little of the agony of crucifixion. In 'Strange Fruit' a 'clearness of the cleansing sun' sums up the equation of nature's ripeness with man's ripening at the coming of war:

> The heart of man has brought to birth
> Splendours richer than his earth.

What is 'strange' is this making of man more natural. In 1914 Binyon had had no chance to hear Billie Holiday sing about the strange fruit of lynched American blacks.

The attempt to cope with the war by cleansing it was tenacious, as can be seen from a sonnet by C.B. Masefield of July 1915. By that time the struggle for Verdun had started and, more significantly for the British, there had been the battles of Neuve Chapelle (10–13 March) and of so-called Second Ypres (28 April). Masefield contrasts the 'two Julys' of his title: July 1914 was a month of vagueness, confusion and worthlessness, while in July 1915 the 'road' is 'so white, so slender' (with interesting intimations of femininity). Power now 'wells in us' and 'we know that every hour/ We must shine brighter, take an edge more keen'.[11] Ironically, Masefield was killed in July 1917. There is no way of knowing how his poem worked for him, and it is commonplace as verse, but it does make clear the appeal of Brookean positions: these give purpose to the carnage and, perhaps, thus protect the sanity of participant and onlooker.

The idea of associating light with the sharp edge of the sword (a weapon which became increasingly anachronistic as the war went on) informs Alfred Noyes's 'The Search-lights' of 1914. Here the lights are originally those of cruisers seeking the enemy. They become probes into human souls ('level shafts of light') and finally a fire which redeems and heals England. The redemption is from 'sloth', 'intellectual pride', 'The trivial jest', 'lawless dreams' and 'cynic Art': a potent and revealing, if faintly nonsensical, brew.[12] Even as late as June 1917 Robert Nichols, in *Ardours and Entrances*, could see the war as 'that mighty winnowing', by which 'Being is blown clean'. This is a force which brings love back 'After grief and shame'; which restores light to the eyes and strength to the hand ('The Day's March'). But the poem is part of a sequence (the title of which is also the volume's) in which individual pieces may have autonomous weight, but where the overall patterning modifies such weight. 'The Day's March' looks back to the start of the war, but it comes early in the sequence and is placed by the later rendering of war's grimness, although it must be added that the closing poems revert to vaguely Brookean mysticism.

The specific challenges of daily life in the war are largely absent from the cleansing poems, while neither Noyes nor Nichols suggests that cleansing may be primarily valuable to the individual personality, rather than (more publicly) to the Army as a whole or to the nation at large. This idea of value to an individual is what makes me reluctant to dismiss a poem like Martin Armstrong's 'Going up the line' of 1918 as routine poeticising or propaganda. Armstrong, educated at Charterhouse and Cambridge, was initially a private in the 2nd Artists Rifles, but was commissioned into the 8th Middlesex in 1915, served on the Western Front, and survived the war. He had published poems before 1914. 'Going up the Line' knows about the war's 'ways of ruin and death', but the poet – like Owen and Sassoon – is conscious that he cannot escape the experience, and the poem finds both 'consolation and refreshment' in 'young Spring'. This enables the poet-figure to 'carry in my soul a power to quell/ All ills and terrors' of the ways of war.[13] Late in the war Armstrong feels able to use such cleansing (and, incidentally, images of bucolic England) as sustaining, but it is striking that it is here so modestly personal. The generalised splendours of Brooke and Binyon are gone.

Brooke had celebrated the coming of war as an event which washed away the dirt of pre-war. A wry coda to such optimism is provided by Corporal Malcolm Hemphrey. His poem 'The New Year' ('East Africa, January 1917'), does not see the war as cleansing. 1916 is dismissed:

> Begone, old year, pass from thy own,
>     And make thou way for newer life;
> Nor grace nor pity will atone
>     For all thy strife.

Despite Hemphrey's awkwardness, his poem sees that the war's experience is too much for grace or pity: atonement can now lie only in some indefinite future:

> some day a greater gale
> Of Hope and Faith shall drive all doubt
> And sharp despair beyond the pale.

Only then will the asphodel 'grace/ The world's lone, ravaged wilderness' and youth be able to 'rest beside the peaceful graves'.[14] When this happens, the dead will be justified: if the war is to prove beneficial, it will be at some vague time in the future, rather than as a cleansing of pre-war.

According to Paul Delany, Brooke welcomed the coming of war as a chance to escape the depression and mess of his private life, and it is plausible to link this with a view of the enthusiasm which greeted the start of the war as being an emotion rooted in relief.[15] The war could be seen as an escape; a chance for the professional military to redeem the failures of the Boer War; an opportunity for male clerks and labourers to escape the tedium of their working lives and impoverished circumstances; more generally, a breakout from the tension of crisis averted or postponed which had marked diplomacy in the long years of peace. If war should prove to be like the chivalric myth or to be dominated by glamorous swords, horses and scarlet tunics, it might prove tonic indeed, a cleansing. But khaki, mud, dull blood-red were to be the colours of this war, and the cleansing of Brooke's sonnets was finally not enough.

Chivalry can be seen as a cleansing of combat, which becomes conceptually possible when warfare is codified, or (more precisely) when training for combat is so ritualised as to be a sport. The training begins to acquire autonomous value, may be practised in its own right, and thereby becomes sport. The history of sport is, broadly, of activities like hunting and fighting being codified in this way and valued in themselves. As early as the sixteenth century, governments showed concern that citizens were interesting themselves in sporting activities with little or no contemporary military value, and by 1600 jousting, for instance, had ceased to have any real connection with battle. Sport became increasingly a product of leisure. In some forms (cricket, varieties of football) its origins seem to be plebeian, connected with carnival or seasonal work-rhythms, but the most relevant development in its history, for our purposes, is genteel: the adoption and high valuing of sport in the so-called public schools of the nineteenth century. Here the emphasis is on self-discipline, corporate endeavour and leadership; and so it is team games that are stressed. For Kipling the appropriate metaphor for the young George Cottar's success as an officer comes from rugby, a version of football which takes its name from Thomas Arnold's school. By 1914 rugby union had purged itself of northern 'professionalism', cricket was firmly under gentry control, and Wimbledon was established as an essentially bourgeois institution. As a profession boxing was plebeian, but strong in the schools as an amateur sport. Jockeys on the flat were also plebeian (partly for physical reasons), but gentry rode 'over the sticks', while owners and Jockey Club stewards were overwhelmingly genteel. Soccer was increasingly a professional and mass sport, but had its public school bastions. 'Corinthian' and 'amateur' were charged terms.

Maurice Keen's account of chivalry is of how the violence and damage of combat were recognised and controlled.[16] Much in the codification of sport can be related to this: the bow is practised by being aimed at non-human targets; the javelin is thrown for distance rather than at another person; feuding between villages becomes ritualised into contests between teams. Within the development of a sport, there may be a similar pattern of limiting violence and restricting physical contact. In boxing, the duration of fights is restricted and so are the areas of the body where blows can be legitimately landed, while in both soccer and the various forms of rugby attempts are made to define acceptable levels of violence. 'Playing by the rules' becomes a test of self-discipline and 'character', but it simultaneously means conforming to a cleansed version of combat or contest. When, therefore, war is represented in terms of sport, it is possible to see the latter as both a cleansed version of the former and as an attempt to cleanse that former. But however powerfully a war/sport analogy may be articulated, it is based upon a lie. In war, killing is legitimate, encouraged: in sport it is accidental, illegitimate. And where the analogy is closest to validity, it is where the realities of war penetrate the codifications of sport – in the infliction of physical damage on your opponent that is the reality behind the rules of boxing and which is not unknown in the scrums of rugby union or among fast bowlers. But the comparisons between war and sport in the poetry of the First World War do not stress this kind of validity; rather, they seek to cleanse war.

One of the best-known accounts of the linking of sport with war is Henry Newbolt's poem 'Vitaï Lampada', wherein the poem's schoolboy is tested in a cricket match. He responds to his captain's appeal, the captain representing both the school and the spirit of the game:

> But his Captain's hand on his shoulder smote –
> 'Play up! play up! and play the game!'

When military crisis comes, the schoolboy has become the captain:

> The river of death has brimmed his banks,
>   And England's far, and Honour a name,
> But the voice of a schoolboy rallies the ranks:
>   'Play up! play up! and play the game!'[17]

Newbolt's hero, it seems, leaves school fully formed, ready to demonstrate the efficacy of his shaping in the 'greater game' of life. But it is worth noting that the refrain makes more of a point than Newbolt may have recognised, for it holds the officer at what should be only a stage towards full development. It would seem from war poems like 'St George's Day: Ypres, 1915' that Newbolt, a non-combatant, found it easy enough to suggest continuity with pre-war:

> Yet say whose ardour bids them stand
>   At bay by yonder bank,
> Where a boy's voice and a boy's hand
>   Close up the quivering rank.
> Who under those all-shattering skies
>   Plays out his captain's part
> With the last darkness in his eyes
>   And *Domum* in his heart?[18]

The unreality of this, in relation to the experience of Ypres, can be seen in the vaguely pastoral 'yonder bank' and in the thought that 'rank' suggests the old world of infantry squares and the 'thin red line', while closing the ranks when troops crossed No Man's Land in the First World War merely meant increased casualties. Also, it is not to deprecate the courage of subalterns to find the suggestion that 'ardour' was the property of officer-boys offensive, as is the intimation that, without their 'boys', the ranks quivered. Patrick Howarth reminds us that Newbolt and Haig were contemporaries at Clifton, and that the former admired what Howarth calls Haig's 'solid athletic merit'.[19] Haig, of course, became the ultimate captain of the British forces.

The strength of 'playing the game' lies in its appeal to a code of behaviour which is known to initiates and does not require analysis. It is an appeal to 'spirit' rather than 'law', which could not easily survive direct experience of the war but which was comfortably available to the editor of *Punch*, Owen Seaman, who was knighted in 1914 and who, in 'Thomas of the Light Heart', sees the ranker as one who 'takes to fighting as a game':

> He'll not disgrace his sporting breed,
> Nor play what isn't cricket. There's his creed.[20]

Seaman's poem is of October 1914, and Seaman was too old to serve in the war. Yet 'the game' is not a concept which was only used by middle-aged outsiders: R.E. Vernède (St Paul's and Oxford) speaks, in 'The Call', of the war as 'the game of games'. Here 'the captains' stress the urgent need of 'a goal' and the volunteer becomes an international:

> Put the old blazer and cap away –
> England's colours await your brow.[21]

Most soldiers, of course, can have had little experience of school blazers and caps, and Vernède's poem remains locked in a minority world.

Such poems provide little detail about particular sports and so the sport/war analogy remains vague, if potent. A good example is Eric Wilkinson's quite lengthy 'Rugby Football' ('written on receiving the Football Match List from Ilkley Grammar School'). Wilkinson, a captain in the West Yorks, won the Military Cross and was killed in action in 1917. His poem, which appears in a section of E.B. Osborn's anthology *The Muse in Arms*, called 'Chivalry of Sport', sees the school as procreator:

> She makes her men and she sends them forth,
> O proud old mother of many sons![22]

These sons are to be found 'Wherever the bond of Empire runs', and their making is associated with rugby, in which 'the fight is clean as a fight should be,/ And they're friends when the ball has ceased to roll'. Wilkinson uses a Newbolt-like refrain: 'Now, School! Now, School! Play up!'. The limitations of the vision of war-as-rugby are obvious enough. The First World War was not clean and, at its end, the antagonists (at least at the level of nations) neither forgot nor forgave. The poem is a protective transformation. Actuality is closer in the verse of Joseph Lee, an NCO in the Black Watch, who had two volumes published by John Murray in 1916 and 1917. Lee is aware of deprivation, dirt, lice and wounds, and has a picture of 'The chaps who stay at home and play/ At tennis through a summer day', but he can still use the sport/war analogy: 'I'd rather play out here!'[23]

The prestige of Newbolt and Seaman suggests that their views of the war as extension of school would be acceptable to the political and social establishment of the early twentieth century; a point which is also made by a poem called 'The Game', by one A. Lockhead, published in *The Times*. This recruitment poem stresses that the war is 'a greater game/ Where worthier deeds are done' than on the football field, and that war is the ultimate democratic sport:

> No game is this where thousands watch
>   The play of a chosen few;
> But rally all! if you're men at all,
>   There's room in the team for you.

Lockhead goes on to itemise the units of the team, ending with the assurance that 'the God of Right will watch the fight,/ And referee the game'.[24] Cate Haste has written of how the Football Association 'put its facilities at the disposal of recruitment bodies' and of how Lord Derby in 1915, closing professional soccer down 'for the duration', exhorted the players of Chelsea and Sheffield United: 'You have played with one another and against one another for the Cup; play with one another for England now.'[25] A curious poem by a certain T. Clayton uses soccer to develop jaunty, humorous patriotism in quite elaborate, if not wholly convincing, Lancashire dialect, stressing that the Germans have been playing dirty. This is what has brought Britain into the war ('For foul play wey conna abide') and Britain will muddle indomitably through:

> Eawr teeom, as yo'know, is a scratched'un;
>   Wey've poiked um up here an'theere;
> But yo'll find every chap as wey've signed on
>   Knows th'best way for th'goalposts to steer.[26]

These examples use team games, drawing on such sports to stress unity, cohesion, team-work and leadership; and they imagine the war effort in such terms. And although, as noticed in passing, they tend to break down as patterns for the actualities of war, it could be said that they offer a grotesque version of reality, imaging the collective anonymity of the serving troops and the terrible power of 'the captains' on the Staff. How the analogy between war and sport is meant to work is beautifully summed up by the epigraph for Captain George Robins' poem 'The Soldier's Game':

> Pluck, endurance, submission to discipline, good temper, calmness, judgement, quickness of observation, self-control, are all qualities as essential in a good polo player as in a good soldier.

This comes, it seems, from the Badminton Library volume on polo. The poem itself emphasises collectivity, 'Never a single selfish stroke,/Every man for the side', and what looks like egalitarianism, 'Rules of precedence too we doff,/Etiquette's self is blind', but polo is a patrician sport and the democracy thereby limited: 'Subalterns ride their Colonel off,/Nor does the Colonel mind'.[27] Robins, however, serves to remind us that the unity of effort which is a striking feature of the war is most convincingly figured as comradeship. His poem provides a version of democracy which is a testimony to the ties of class and school among officers. Rankers are absorbed into this, but the poem is another effort at transformation, achieving this, however, only by eliding the antagonisms between Front and Staff and between regulars and volunteers – antagonisms which blurred class divisions and created unions which Robins ignores.

It is, however, the case that, given the mass of verse which survives the war, the comparison between war and sport is not particularly common. Among combatants, in fact, it becomes a rarity. The pattern will simply not sustain or stand up to the experience – a point made by failures of the analogy, as seen above. It can express limited points of comparison sharply enough, as in W.W. Gibson's 'Sport' which compares war with cubbing. War is seen as a healthy outdoor activity: and the enemy are only different to the cubs in being 'crueller, craftier game'.[28] Even here the alleged cruelty of cubs is dubious and, of course, cubs are not very dangerous. It might be added that the war/sport analogy is not one which seems to have had much appeal to the most highly-regarded poets of the war; not even as an object of parody or satire.

In so far, then, as the comparison between war and sport breaks down and is relatively neglected in poetry of the First World War it can be suggested that the effort to cleanse war by means of analogy fails. Such examples as Newbolt's 'Vitaï Lampada' and Kipling's story 'The Brushwood Boy', however, remind us that the analogy was established long before 1914 and that it is rooted in a relationship between the two phenomena which is historically valid. The dominant conditions of the First World War subverted the traditional relationship because these conditions were simply incompatible with what was seen as the essence of sport. War has probably never been sporting, but sport itself has been more obviously brutal in past centuries. Changes in the nature of both elements made the relationship untenable in 1914–18.

The sonnets of Rupert Brooke, with which this chapter began, are synthetic, in that they draw together attitudes which are not Brooke's invention to represent an ideological pattern which can be seen as a preparation for war. But this preparation takes the form of myth-making of a kind which suppresses or cleanses actuality to enable action. Yet although the deficiencies of the myth are evident enough now, we should never underestimate the power of lies and half-lies: and the foot-prints of Rupert Brooke are ubiquitous in the verse of the First World War. We have already seen something of this, but the impact is also observable in the widespread tendency to rely on harmonious generalisations which evade and discourage recognition of reality. So Herbert Asquith opens a poem called 'War's Cataract' with a lofty response to the scale of the phenomenon ('this red havoc of the patient earth') but his sonnet registers nothing of the detail of this. It alleges some kind of facing of reality ('Now has the hero cast away disguise') but purifies what is alleged:

> out of ruin splendour comes to birth.
> This is the field where Death and Honour meet.[29]

What is at stake here is not a simple issue of truth and lies so much as the consequences of Asquith's glibness. There is no need to deny that something that could be called 'splendour' did show itself in the courage of soldiers, or that many died honourably. But Asquith's lines erase effort, are seductive – and in that sense dangerous – both in encouraging a narcotic response in a reader and in revealing a numbed brain in the writer. The Brooke of the war sonnets encouraged such narcosis.

Asquith's poem ends with the image of rainbows meeting the day through and above the darkness of thunder, while Aubrey Herbert speaks of Brooke as 'rainbow comrade' in his elegy for the dead poet.[30] In a sense, Herbert's Brooke is aptly seen as a rainbow, a radiance shining against a dark sky, for in Herbert's poem Brooke is a bright, sharp presence: a cleanness. The image of his 'clear singing, clean as is the swimmer's joy' is close to Brooke's own 'swimmers into cleanness leaping' ('Peace'), and Herbert's Brooke is a bard with 'golden harpstrings' who 'sang the knightly truth'. This chivalric Brooke offered a truth which embraced both Homeric epic and English Arthurian myth, and what is mourned is the loss of Brooke as a 'recorder' of this 'fight of ours'. It is important to notice that Herbert suggests that what Brooke would have recorded would have been rendered in terms of 'visions of the springtime, Holy Grail and Golden Fleece'. There is, however, no suggestion that this would have included the sense, found in Homer and Malory alike, of the filth and brutality of war. But Herbert is not concerned with mundane truth. He writes of Brooke as singing of the 'light of Greece' and of how he drank 'the wine . . . of battle', and he stresses the dead poet's youth. Brooke is not the poet of Greece; he knew little about battle; and he was hardly a youth when he died. Brooke, the maker of myths, is himself made into a myth.

Ivor Gurney dedicated his five 'Sonnets 1917' to the memory of Rupert Brooke.[31] The dedication has its irony. The sonnets were published in Gurney's first volume of poems (*Severn and Somme*, 1917) and contain clear reminders of Brooke in, for instance, their patriotism ('If it were not for England, who would bear/ This heavy servitude one moment more?') and in some phrasings: 'giving all in one white glow', 'Thy love . . . Whereto the power of Death's destruction is weak'. But Gurney is not writing an elegy for Brooke, and, if the latter's example can be said to lie behind Gurney's poems, the tribute is in the quality of what Gurney has made; the irony being that he has gone far beyond Brooke.

Whatever Gurney's purpose may have been, he has clearly established the grounds for comparison: his poems are sonnets, as Brooke's had been; he also groups five poems; and his title echoes Brooke's simple '1914'. The differences, however, begin to emerge if the titles of the two quintets are compared. Brooke's poems are called, in order, 'Peace', 'Safety', 'The Dead', 'The Dead' (again), and 'The Soldier'. Gurney's titles are 'For England', 'Pain', 'Servitude', 'Home-sickness' and 'England the Mother'. He has nothing equivalent to 'Peace' or 'Safety' (except perhaps in associations of 'England'), while Brooke has nothing like 'Pain' or 'Servitude' (except perhaps in associations of 'Dead'). But the important differences are of experience, complexity and capacity for thought. From the beginning of the first sonnet it should be clear that Gurney is thinking rather than musing. So the possible 'joy-bewildering/ Pleasures' of heaven are set against 'Earth's mortal loveliness' in a genuine contest of values, and the poem's thoughtful sense of conflict is marked in the phrasing of the sestet's opening:

> So the dark horror clouds us, and the dread
> Of the unknown . . . But if it must be, then
> What better passing than to go out like men
> For England, giving all in one white glow?

The recognition of 'the dread/Of the unknown', the qualifications of 'But . . . then', and the starkness of 'go out' make for a complex which in turn means that 'one white glow' is much more than a Brookean phrase. The complex makes, in fact, a comment upon Brooke.

The opening of 'Pain' is well beyond Brooke's grasp, in its confident repetition and in Gurney's typical discrimination:

> Pain, pain continual; pain unending;
> Hard even to the roughest, but to those
> Hungry for beauty. . . .

In the same poem Gurney unites man and animal without sentimentality or any urge to make a moral point:

> the pitiful eyes of men foredone,
> Or horses shot, too tired merely to stir,
> Dying in shell-holes both, slain by the mud.
> Men broken, shrieking even to hear a gun.

This is precious, particular knowledge – the fatigue, the horrible bathos of dying in mud, the recognition of the broken men (some of whom were shot as cowards). There is much more: the brilliant summary of ranker-experience as 'this brass-cleaning life'; the pride of the individual 'Harried in foolishness, scanned curiously o'er/By fools made brazen by conceit'; the levelling humour of 'such boys/ As neither brass nor Hell-fire may appal,/Nor guns, nor sergeant-major's bluster and noise' (all from 'Servitude'). There is an individual intimacy in these sonnets which emerges beautifully in the pause and identification here:

> O tiny things, but very stuff of soul

To us . . . so frail . . . Remember what we are. . . .

('Home-sickness')

It is such detailing which anchors these sonnets, so that when the final poem of what is a real sequence claims 'We have done our utmost, England' the claim is moving because it is informed by a specific sense of that doing, as something which embraces extreme fatigue, broken human beings, brass-cleaning and being 'scanned curiously'. Moreover, Gurney's patriotism is thereby a complex entity: as 'mother' England is 'terrible/And dear'; as rural it is itemised but not decorated ('Blackbird, bluebell, hedge-sparrow, tiny daisies'); and, in 'Servitude', it becomes, in effect, one's comrades. 'Servitude' begins with a question about enduring, to which the answer is 'England'. But the sestet, which asserts in parallel that 'Only the love of comrades sweetens all', works, I think, to define England as essentially such comrades.

I have emphasised Gurney's particularity, and the detailed recording of war experience is very important as part of the necessary testing of the lies and half-truths out of which wars come. But it would be misleading to suggest that Gurney is a naturalistic poet, to be set against an idealist Brooke. Brooke cleansed his war sonnets of the specificity of his own best pre-war verse, and this facilitates the operation of these poems as propaganda. Gurney seems unable, when writing well, to purge particularity, and this is a strength; but it is not because he has no sense of ideals or lacks a feeling for generalisation. He can operate movingly with the latter, as the octet of 'For England' shows, and he can move tellingly from detail to summary response, as he does in 'Pain', where the last line has an appalling transcendence of the preceding detail:

The amazed heart cries angrily out on God.

What Gurney achieves in these sonnets matters for this chapter for an obvious, but important, reason. His achievement is a refusal to cleanse and a commentary on the final deceitfulness of cleansing the inevitable dirt and squalor of the physics and metaphysics of war. All that is cleansed is brass.

## NOTES

1. *The Poems*, ed. T. Rogers, Black Swan, 1987.
2. ibid. p. 26.

3. For the relationship of this to Brooke's own experiences see Paul Delany, *The Neo-Pagans*, Macmillan, 1987.
4. ibid. p. 95.
5. From the second 'The Dead' sonnet ('These hearts were woven . . .').
6. Watson, *Collected Poems*, p. 217.
7. Adcock, p. 46.
8. *The New Elizabethans*, John Lane, 1919, pp. 6, 98–9.
9. ibid. p. 308.
10. In *Poetry of the Great War*, ed. D. Hibberd and J. Onions, Macmillan, 1986, pp. 110–11.
11. In *More Songs by the Fighting Men*, Erskine MacDonald, 1917, p. 102.
12. In *A Treasury of War Poetry*, ed. G.H. Clarke, Houghton Mifflin, 1917, pp. 99–100.
13. In *Up the Line to Death*, ed. B. Gardner (1964), Magnum, 1976, p. 119.
14. *More songs.* . . . pp. 66–7.
15. Delany, p. 209.
16. *Chivalry*, Yale University Press, 1984.
17. Newbolt, *Collected Poems*, pp. 131–3.
18. *Poems Old and New*, Murray, 1919, pp. 89–90.
19. *Play Up and Play the Game*, Eyre Methuen, 1973, p. 7.
20. *A Treasury.* . . . pp. 131–2.
21. In *Poetry of the First World War*, ed. M. Hussey (1971), Longman, 1976, pp. 139–41.
22. *The Muse in Arms*, ed. E.B. Osborn, Murray, 1918, pp. 208–11.
23. ' "Stay-at-home hearts are best" – not 'alf!', in *Ballads of Battle*, Murray, 1916, pp. 50–2.
24. In *Songs and Poems of the Great World War*, ed. D. Tulloch, Davis Press, 1915, pp. 55–6.
25. *Keep the Home Fires Burning*, Allen Lane, 1977.
26. 'Call it a draw', Tulloch, pp. 225–6.
27. Osborn, *The Muse in Arms*, Murray, 1916, pp. 195–7.
28. *Battle*, Elkin Mathews, 1916, p. 18.
29. Osborn, p. 144.
30. 'R.B.', ibid. p. 128.
31. *Severn and Somme/War's Embers*, ed. R.K. Thornton, MidNag/Carcanet, 1987.

# 3

# SATIRE AND SIEGFRIED SASSOON

The idea of war as a cleansing agent allows positive values to be expressed, especially as attributes of your own side. Courage, self-sacrifice, honour can be celebrated, using images which are themselves purifications – 'playing the game', being chivalric, being Christ-like. Such cleansing is likely to appeal to those who are controlling and organising the war effort and it will be promoted by such people as positive propaganda which, if effective, works as sympathetic magic. The projection of positive images of the race and its cause may thus help the war effort in various ways, these being summed up as encouraging individuals to live up to the image directed at them. The technique is that of Shakespeare's Henry V before Harfleur and it is conveniently illustrated by John Arkwright's poem 'The Civilian', designed, it would seem, to make the clerkly civilian believe that 'He too had carried a sword'.[1]

The negative to this is propaganda formally directed at the enemy. Clearly, positive propaganda works by attributing unqualified virtue to, for example, the race or nation or to groups within race or nation. Equally obviously, negative propaganda works by denigrating those it is directed at. It reduces its targets to disgusting elementals, by denying to the individuals or nation under attack the attributes commonly held to distinguish humankind. Such propaganda may be actually targeted upon its formal objects, or it may denigrate them while being addressed to the nation or group the propagandist supports, working to encourage their sense of righteousness by showing them negative images of their opponents. But, whether the actual audience of negative propaganda is its ostensible object or an ally of the propagandist, the dominant method of such propaganda remains that of satire.

Cate Haste makes the point that 'The essence of propaganda is simplification'[2], and this applies both to negative and positive propaganda. Censorship also relates to both. The image of Rupert Brooke that can be seen as positive propaganda for a purified and inspiring young England is that of Edward Marsh's hagiographic memoir,[3] which censors out the intellectual snobbery, the anti-Semitism and sexual nastiness most marked in the period of Brooke's breakdown.[4] Conversely, the propagandist effort of the Bryce Report on alleged German atrocities (1915) uses selection and censorship to produce what is, in effect, a satire on the German character. Such an effect can be achieved even with an obstensibly neutral medium such as photography, as is obvious to anyone who looks at the photographic 'histories' of the war. On page 33 of volume five of the Amalgamated Press *War Illustrated*,[5] for example, there is a photograph of German prisoners, looking weary and dejected. The caption makes the propagandist point: 'The dejection of failure only emphasizes the animal sullenness of their heavy faces' (faces which are, in fact, resigned and tired rather than anything else). Positive and negative propaganda are meant to interlock or trans-refer. As you look at your enemy's 'animal sullenness' you are to think of yourself as its opposite; as, say, Schell's photograph of Rupert Brooke or an idealised picture of Florence Nightingale.

At the beginning of the war, satire's most obvious target was, of course, the enemy. Since the declaration of war was popular, satire could perhaps have no other target of any significance except for minorities sceptical about the motives behind the declaration or opposed to war itself. Such minorities were themselves potential targets for satire, but were only significant later, when their nuisance value was felt. Meanwhile, Bertram Dobell's *Songs and Lyrics on the War* shows how anti-German satire could be constructed.[6]

Dobell died in December 1914 and his volume is an example of early non-combatant response to the coming of war. It exemplifies well the trans-referential dimension of propaganda mentioned above. Britain is seen as the champion of freedom, its soldiers being 'True offspring of your dauntless sires of old!' ('To our soldiers'). The effort of Britain and its allies is the struggle against a Germany which is satirised as 'feudal' and 'barbarian'. So Dobell calls easily upon the idea of the German nation as the reanimation of the Teutons of the past, those swarms of Goths, Huns and Vandals which brought down the glory of Rome and introduced the Dark Ages. Dobell has to forget that the Allies were scarcely free of such blood. For him the modern 'hordes' are merely 'Prussian' (reducing

the racial and historical complexity of greater Germany to the
Prussian element, with its ready associations of militarism and
aggression). Germany is personified as 'Attila' ('The tragedy of a
nation') and its culture is 'The law of Attila' renewed ('The
destruction of Louvain'). Frederick the Great is simply a
'freebooter', 'Nietzsche and Treischke' are 'unmelodious names . . .
of evil omen', while Goethe and Heine are, in effect, denaturalised.[7]
So Germans have to be dehumanised and isolated:

> bestial creatures in the shape of men;
> One land alone this mongrel progeny breeds –
> Kin to the tribes that herd in cave and den.
>
> ('The Prussian Atrocities')

Dobell's attacks show little precision or thought, and the knee-jerk
nature of his satire occurs in other writers. Studdert Kennedy (who
served at the Front as a padre), savaging the idea of a god of power,
links such a god with those 'who would stand and watch a Hun/Ram
his bayonet through the bowels of a baby just for fun' ('High and
lifted up').[8] Here the main object of attack is this version of God, but
the reference to the Hun is a shorthand exploitation of propaganda to
draw out a stock response. Another priest, Henry Lovelady, vicar of
Oldham, sees the Belgians as giving 'their lands for the Huns to
tread,/Their homes for the Huns to burn'.[9] The repeated 'Huns'
sums up the sense of barbarian hordes to produce the easy negative
response. Mary Symon associates Hell and Hun to construct an
imprecise apocalypse:

> Hell is loose
> Across yon strip of sea;
> Its trampling hordes are at our gates –
> Once in, and what are we?
> The helots of the Hun accurst. . . .
>
> ('A Call to Arms')[10]

Just after the end of the war, Gilbert Frankau, in a poem called
'Poison', attacks those who call for forgiveness of the Germans by
invoking the idea that this enemy will not change:

> Fools! Shall the pard change his skin
>     Or cleanse one spot from it?
> As the lecher returns to his sin
>     So the cur to its vomit.
>     Fools! Hath the Hun
> Earned place in the sun?[11]

But such examples of direct and rather crude exploitation of stock reactions are less common than might be expected.

A more oblique satirical technique is to expose the enemy in what purport to be his own words. The best examples I have come across belong to Tulloch's anthology, *Songs and Poems of the Great World War*. There are a number of anti-German poems in this book, including parodies and verses which use popular metres. Quite a few of these employ humour rather than direct satire:

> Why grudge the mild and gentle Hun
>   His right to gambol in the sun?
>                     (R. Arkwell, 'By Wireless from Berlin')

> The other night, after a bout
> With leberwurst and sauerkraut,
> I slept the sleep of just and true,
> As Attila the Great would do. . . .
>                     (A.W.H., 'The Kaiser's Dream')

> . . . we'd haul down the Union Jack
>   And hoist the German Vulture,
> And every English town we'd sack
>   To show our German culture!
>                     (M.B.H., 'The Calais of our Ally')[12]

Tulloch's volume is itself propaganda, and it contains some quite gruesome patriotism, as well as a certain amount of crude anti-German writing, but its chief satirical device is a kind of ridicule that delights in making the enemy seem foolish rather than vicious. This is something that links such verses with soldiers' songs rather than with the hectic voice of a 'serious' poet such as Dobell.

Siegfried Sassoon is remembered as *the* satirical poet of the war, and of the war's better-known poets he is the one who is most consistently satirical of aspects of war experience. But several points need to be made about Sassoon's satire, and how this came to be his dominant mode.

Sassoon was not a satirist before the war. The version of self he fictionalises as the pre-war George Sherston is essentially one of ignorance and philistinism: and this exercise in fictional autobiography can be seen as nostalgic satire, with Sherston's immersion in the war reflecting on his Edwardian innocence. But Sassoon himself was neither as ignorant nor as philistine as Sherston. He had the formal education of the privileged (Marlborough and Cambridge), was 28 at the beginning of the war and had been writing poems for some years – poems marked by various influences and some cultural experience, but no marked tendency to either satire or disillusionment. He enlisted in the Sussex Yeomanry in August 1914, was commissioned in the Royal Welsh Fusiliers in May 1915 and was with that regiment's first battalion in France in November. He was awarded the Military Cross in June 1916 and was not officially retired from the army until March 1919. The period of his service was marked by gallantry (which earned him the nickname 'Mad Jack') and, as is widely known, by wounds, breakdown and the famous protest against the war which led to his committal to the hospital at Craiglockhart. Sassoon was a successful soldier, if success is applied courage, and a success for the army, in so far as it managed to contain his rebellion and retain his services. And although *The Old Huntsman*, which contains satirical poems like ' "Blighters" ' and 'They', was published in 1917, and *Counter-Attack* in June 1918, Sassoon was not a prominent poet of the war while it was going on. Since he survived, he scarcely qualifies for inclusion in Adcock's *For Remembrance*, but he is a minor figure in contemporary anthologies: absent from *More Songs. . .* and G.H. Clarke's *Treasure of War Poetry*; represented in Osborn's *The Muse in Arms* by the early and non-satirical 'Absolution' and the 'realist' 'The Rear-guard', and in Trotter's *Valour and Vision* by three short pieces ('Dreamers', 'Attack' and 'Remorse') which, while clearly not pro-war, are yet not directly satirical of it.

But if Sassoon did not go to war as a satirist, he quickly became one. 'Absolution', of April–September 1915, is Brookean, with its themes of absolution, the shining out of beauty and the war as a scourge which brings wisdom and freedom, but Sassoon's own retrospective note pins the poem down as a typical early response: 'People used to feel like this when they "joined up" in 1914 and 1915. No one feels it when they "go out again" '.[13] His dates suggest that people who 'went out again' quickly began to feel the confusion, exhaustion and pressure which he catches in 'The Redeemer', but that poem is not satirical, and several others follow before 'In the Pink', of February 1916. Sassoon says that the *Westminster Review* rejected this latter poem 'as they thought it might prejudice recruiting!!'. The Davies of the poem is ignorant and doomed:

To-night he's in the pink; but soon he'll die.
And still the war goes on – he don't know why.

But this weariness and lack of known purpose constitute potential rather than actual satire.

Poems seem to have come in rapid succession for Sassoon in 1916, and they quickly begin to show revision of the values and ideals of the war's beginning. There is observation of the unpleasant – 'the brown rats, the nimble scavengers' of 'Golgotha' – and the sardonic contrast in 'A Subaltern' between earlier summer days (with a parody of Newbolt – 'twenty runs to make, and last man in') and the rats, slime and 'palsied weather' of this 'Hell'. The writing comes close to satire at times:

> O Jesus, send me a wound to-day,
> And I'll believe in Your bread and wine,
> And get my bloody old sins washed white!
>
> ('Stand-to: Good Friday Morning')

There is identification with the enemy ('A Night Attack'); the sardonic acceptance of amputation as a release from the fighting ('The One-Legged Man'); and, in 'The Death-Bed', a moment when the poet begins to set his satirical sights:

> He's young; he hated War; how should he die
> When cruel old campaigners win safe through?

Sassoon notes that this poem was 'Refused by the *Westminster* without comment'.

A common theme of Adcock's *For Remembrance* is that the young men of his account did not like war, and this can be linked with the idea that Britain was anxious to avoid conflict. War is forced upon the nation, but is made acceptable because the cause is good and war can be a cleansing. Sassoon's poems, however, move to satire as he registers no cleansing and the physical and psychological cost which is being exacted. The satire comes out of the experiential pressure which is its validification; and it comes to seem the inevitable result of that pressure. Two or three preliminary points should be made. The first is that the detail of the accounts of trench experience provides the justification for satire (which is not to say that the targets of his satire are necessarily and always the most appropriate ones); the second, that Sassoon does not satirise the military enemy (who, where treated, are seen as suffering in the same situation); the third, that Sassoon's poems do not satirise either ranker or subaltern.

There is no reason to believe that Sassoon was a pacifist in 1914 or that he was then opposed to this particular war. The poems also suggest that his movement to satire was emotional rather than intellectual: the response to the physical conditions of the trenches leads to questioning of why and how the suffering is going on. The Sherston of *Memoirs of a Fox-hunting Man*, being both ignorant and unreflective, goes unquestioningly to war, and would seem to be an accurate figuring – perhaps mildly satirised – of Sassoon's own condition in 1914. The awakening caused by blood, mud and shell, and the satirical questioning which follows are visceral rather than cerebral. It is this that makes Sassoon's best satire a convincing version of the resentment of combatants which, in collective terms, was most forcefully expressed in the mutiny in the Etaples Bull Ring (1917–18).

The first fully satirical poem (following the dating in *The War Poems*) is 'They', of 31 October 1916, and it is centred on one of Sassoon's chief themes, the gap between Home and Front. Its two stanzas present two speakers. The first is the bishop, an Establishment figure based, so Sassoon's note tells us, on the bishop of London. This bishop speaks of a transformation which 'the boys' will experience, 'for they'll have fought/In a just cause'. Daring death and attacking anti-Christ, they, because of the sacrificial blood of their dead comrades, have 'New right to breed an honourable race'. This bland and confident vision is brutally contrasted with the reply of 'the boys', in which transformation is into disablement:

> "For George lost both his legs; and Bill's stone blind;
> Poor Jim's shot through the lungs and like to die;
> And Bert's gone syphilitic. . . ."

The bishop's only reply is that 'The ways of God are strange!'. The bishop speaks of a Brookean awakening, but this is no longer a combatant vision, and the poem marks a chasm between the crude facts of physical disablement and the bishop's brand of Christianity. The impact made derives largely from contrast, together with the implication that the bishop is impervious to the voices of 'the boys', but the brutality of the contrast is elsewhere presented more frontally, as in ' "Blighters" ', of February 1917. If the bishop was unnamed and given no character except by implication, the target of this poem – Music Hall performers and audience – is attacked with fierce detail: an audience which grins and cackles, 'while prancing ranks/Of harlots shrill the chorus, drunk with din'. The chorus is imagined as singing 'We're sure the Kaiser loves our dear old Tanks!'; and it is such a tank which the poem would 'like to see . . .

come down the stalls' to stop jokes seen as mocking 'the riddled corpses round Bapaume'. The heightened language pushes towards the dismissiveness of 'harlots' and there is again the marking of the gap between the jaunty 'dear old Tanks!' and the grim 'riddled corpses'. But the gap, the poem imagines, could be closed by a tank in the Music Hall, and this brings ' "Blighters" ' close to 'Fight to a Finish', which was written from Craiglockhart in 1917, after Sassoon's protest against the war. This poem uses the idea of soldiers returning from the war to a ceremonial reception, this being seen as the apotheosis of 'all the thrills and ardours' of the conflict. But the soldiers charge the mob and the poet-figure enters the poem in its last three lines to hear the grunts and squeals of the 'Yellow-Pressmen' and to go with his 'trusty bombers' to clear 'those Junkers out of Parliament'. The fight to a finish of the title indicates that the final battle is with Home: chauvinism has been fully reversed. The attack is general ('the mob') but with particulars included – the popular press (the language of which elevates and distorts the experience of the war) and Parliament (where Sassoon's protest had made little impact). There is the further suggestion that this final military task is a push-over ('At last the boys had found a cushy job'), while 'Junkers', in the last line, drives home the point that the real enemy is at Home.

Poem upon poem repeats the theme of alienation and, collectively, the picture is filled in. So 'Glory of Women' savagely suggests that women get a sexual thrill from 'tales of dirt and danger' and that they cannot (blinded with ideas of chivalry and laurel) believe that British soldiers retreat or, more precisely, 'run/, Trampling the terrible corpses – blind with blood'. In 'Remorse', which is, mockingly, a sonnet, the body of the poem details trench horrors ('swamp and welter. . .flounders. . .gloom. . .Screaming. . .stumps. . .Livid with terror, clutching. . .sticking 'em like pigs. . . ') in a typical Sassoon lexicon. Then the poem's persona reflects upon what cannot be told to 'Poor father sitting safe at home, who reads/Of dying heroes and their deathless deeds'. 'Poor' may suggest some sympathy, but Sassoon's usual attitude to such security as this father has is contempt ('Base Details'). 'Suicide in the Trenches' starkly marks the breaking of simplicity in two short stanzas, while the third turns to

> You smug-faced crowds with kindling eye
> Who cheer when soldier lads march by,

Sneak home and pray you'll never know
The hell where youth and laughter go.

A reading of Sassoon's poems of the war makes the point that Home includes almost everything which is not Trench. Staff is thus part of Home, being seen as an aspect of the callous, unknowing attitudes which are excoriated in Sassoon's satire. The 'scarlet Majors at the Base' in 'Base Details' are secure: they 'speed glum heroes up the line to death', but themselves guzzle in good hotels; the general of the poem is no part of its 'we' and his 'plan of attack' is murderous.

This suggests that the voices of Sassoon's poems of the war are to be seen as representing the reactions of combatants. Something like this is indicated by the blurring of the lines between ranker and subaltern. The personae and other individual soldiers may be either, but the reactions remain the same; and Sassoon's satirical style makes use of a direct idiom, which can be seen as classless (although this is finally a delusion, since Sassoon's is an educated style). The point is that the pressures of the war on combatants are seen as creating comradeship (something which readily includes the enemy). The poems implicitly claim that they speak for all who fight, and this is true even to the extent that they show little interest in discriminating and – specifically – little interest in representing the particular responses of particular ranks. Experience, it is suggested, produces uniformity.

The poems say that their poet and his fictional characters have come to oppose this war because they have lost faith in it. This does not make them pacifist poems. The 'message' of ' "Blighters" ' and 'Fight to a Finish' is of applying the violence learnt in the war to those at home. This is not, however, proposed in terms of a defined political policy or of an analysis of the causes of the war. Sassoon's socialism was as shallow as Brooke's and the programme of 'Fight to a Finish' is sub-philosophical militaristic anarchy. There is little analysis of causes, although the gap which is articulated between Home and combatant hints that the war is the product of slogans about honour and chivalry. Such slogans, the poems say, come to have no meaning for soldiers, because of the obscene details of combatant experience. The implication is that these details, if fully understood, should stop this war and prevent others, because 'riddled corpses' outweigh all other considerations. As an analysis this is utterly understandable but sadly insufficient. It could only work if it were universally appreciated, and the history of the decades since 1918 says that that has not happened: the battlefields of the Iran/Iraq war are much like those of Ypres and the Somme.

This implies something about Sassoon's strengths and weaknesses; and also something about satiric war poetry. An aesthetic reading of Sassoon's verse is a disgusting idea. The crudeness of his effects and the iteration of foul detail are necessary parts of the attitudes being conveyed: the poet is driven to hoarseness, repetition and brutality by the deafness which keeps the war going. In so far as the verse is sickening it is proper: vomit may be necessary. But while vomiting may be enough to cope with mild toxification, it cannot purge strong poison. Paradoxically, the desperation of Sassoon's satire may even perpetuate war, because what is articulated is as impatient of analysis as that which the satire attacks. The anger of the alienated soldier deserves more respect than the ideals-masked callousness of 'the mob', but if the produce of that anger is 'trusty bombers' clearing Parliament by force, the solution replicates the problem. In terms, therefore, of the 'task' of poetry of the First World War, Sassoon's satire was necessary but not enough.

Satire commonly expresses or pretends strong emotion, but it can also be intellectually analytic, as the satiric writing of Ben Jonson and John Dryden shows. Satire is, by definition, partisan. Negative propaganda uses satire on behalf of one party by distorting the attitudes of opponents, and it is seldom squeamish about its methods. Sassoon's negatives are to be set against the pictures of the suffering combatants, and the effort is to make the contrasts as sharp as possible (this often being stressed by breaks in the text). These contrasts, as we have seen, are usually between Trench and Home. This may be set against the Allies/Enemy contrast which was basic to both negative and positive propaganda but which is missing in Sassoon's work. But a satiric account which seeks to destroy Home totally (seeing all women as harlots, all fathers as secure in illusion) can only rely on Trench, which isolates, corrupts and teaches violence. 'The Kiss' (April 1916) may be a satire on bayonet-fixation, or it may be part of Sassoon's early acceptance of the war, but in either case it reads as if relishing the clean violence of the weapon, and the same may be said of 'Fight to a Finish'. Ambivalence and a lack of analysis are central to Sassoon's satire, but contempt and hatred are antagonistic, matching blindness with blindness:

> Lost in the swamp and welter of the pit,
> He flounders. . . .

In 1927–8 Sassoon wrote 'On passing the New Menin Gate', a
sonnet which ends:

> Well might the Dead who struggled in the slime
> Rise and deride this sepulchre of crime.

Emotionally, this is proper. Sanity says that it must be a crime to kill
so many, but by 1928 the Nazis were within four years of becoming
the largest party in the Reichstag. Fascists often had distinguished
war records, and were not averse to bombers and fixed bayonets as
agents of 'cleansing'. Sassoon's kind of satire should have worked to
prevent such things, but the satirist's perennial problem is how to
get people to recognise themselves in the satirical mirror.

Sassoon's technique of satiric contrast makes use of the conditions of
the combatant, setting these against the attitudes and behaviour of
Home. This version of combatant experience is cognate with those
Sassoon poems which are 'reportage' rather than satire. His
reportage poems offer a journalistic alternative to the Yellow Press
(and, one might add, to much of the 'quality' press as well) and they
are not satirical in any direct sense. Yet their use of concentrated and
revolting detail, violently expressed, is close to satire, even though
this does not involve satirisation of the figures described. What is
satirical is seeing such conditions as the product of Home attitudes,
with the possible further satirical implication that the victims
(including the I-figures) are fools to continue. Sassoon's war poems,
as a whole, provide the most sustained allegation that there is a
connection between the conditions of the combatants and indifference at home. But such topics concerned other poets of the war.

T.B. Clark's volume, *Poems of a Private*, is very conscious of
Home.[14] The cover of my copy says that the volume ('A souvenir of
France and Salonica') has been 'Presented to, Accepted, and
Acknowledged by Royalty', while the author's note claims that the
poems 'portray "Tommy" in his true colours, and express his own
point of view', this including 'high spirits and never-failing cheerfulness' as well as 'a deeper note that thrills his life'. One or two poems
have explanatory notes for non-combatants, while others seem
specifically directed at Home ('Commentary on Rations'). Clark is
not a 'literary' writer, but handles popular verse forms quite
confidently. The head-note to 'Tommy's Troubles' suggests that the
poem could be sung, and Clark's usual style employs rousing,

strongly-marked rhythms. But one of his themes is cheerful grumbling about conditions, this producing the satire of 'Commentary on Rations':

> Tea and sugar's very scarce,
> And the butter even worse,
> Maconachie's a total loss,
> Unless you chance to win the toss;
> A full grown navvy could devour
> A section's bacon in an hour. . . .

Or there is the use of litotes in 'Tommy's Troubles':

> If your billet's not attractive,
> Make allowances for 'Active';
> Though it isn't very nice
> When you sleep with rats and mice,
> To say nothing of the lice;
> Never mind.

But the volume, taken as a whole, suggests that Tommy's grumbling is of the Bairnsfather variety – a part of the lovable persona of the ranker and not to be taken too seriously. Conditions may be bad, but the private soldier shows a cheerful pride –

> We will strafe them from their trenches,
>     And they'll wish themselves in clover,
> When we're bombing their defences,
>     With our 'Special' whizzing over.

('The Strafing Section')

– and resilience:

> There are hardships to contend,
> But the War is bound to end;
> And the Germans you must kill.

('Tommy's Troubles')

Clark's poems read like deliberate attempts to project the poet as 'Tommy', and the collective emphasis would be reassuring to Home, except at the end of 'Commentary on Rations', where a threatening note troubles the cheerfulness:

> I say it is a beastly shame,
> And that they do not play the game;
> While the Kaiser's Huns you smash,
> To serve you with such awful trash;
> I'd like to put a nasty 'twist'
> On Kaiser Bill and his mailed fist.

Apart from such a moment, where Clark sounds a little like Sassoon, his satire is that of carnival and the court jester. The grumbling is the complainer's way of letting off steam, and is not any cause for anxiety. Tommy seems to be coping pretty well.

In his memoir *Undertones of War* Edmund Blunden adopts the persona of a 'harmless shepherd' who goes innocent to war, like Sassoon's Sherston.[15] Blunden was, in fact, a public school pupil who survived the war. He fought on the Somme and at Ypres, winning the Military Cross, but his poems of the war (which will be more closely looked at in a later chapter) do not follow Sassoon into satire, nor did he make a public protest against the war. Yet Blunden does show a satirical streak – one which demonstrates his sense of the conditions under which the fighting was done and which also indicates some alienation from Home. But Blunden's satirical contrasts are usually more oblique than Sassoon's and historical rather than sociological. So the 'senseless rage' which is the experience of war in 'Les Halles D'Ypres' is set against history:

> Only the foursquare tower still bears the trace
> Of beauty that was, and strong embattled age.[16]

'La Quinque Rue' places memory, tradition and moonlight's powers of transformation against the realities of war:

> . . . surely now the grounds both left and right
> Are tilled, and scarless houses undismayed
> Glow in the lustrous mercy of sweet night. . .
> Why lead me then
> Through the foul-gorged, the cemeterial fen
> To fear's sharp sentries?

'Preparations for Victory' is a sardonic version of the tradition of debates between body and soul, but also between the expectations of literary tradition and the dreadful pressure of actuality.

Blunden's poetry has a deep sanity about it which is impressive even where the style is mannered or contorted. It is a sanity of remembering pasts and holding to them even in the midst of destruction, but it is also at times the sanity of the absurdist, as in 'The Guard's Mistake'. Here the company responds to finding a billet in undamaged territory with pleasure:

> We halted, and were glad; the country lay
> After our marching, like a sabbath day.

The location calls for severance from the war:

> And when the guard was at the main gate set,
> Surrounding pastoral urged them to forget.

An 'ill-omened' royal visit, however, restores 'reality':

> The crimson-mottled monarch, shocked and shrill,
> Sent our poor sentry scampering for his gun,
> Made him once more 'the terror of the Hun'.

It is difficult to imagine Blunden writing like the Brooke of 'Peace' or 'The Soldier', but it is also hard to believe that he could or would attempt the direct brutalities of Sassoon. Yet Blunden's feeling for discrepancies is acute, whereby the war is seen as constantly articulating breaks with the past. The war does this of its very nature, rather than because it exemplifies the greed or guilt of either side. Blunden is concerned with effects rather than causes. These effects include the satirical observation of a new type of sowing in 'Rural Economy', which uses a new 'Bone-fed loam' to bring 'a roaring harvest home', and the satirical use of 'this old guide-book to the Netherlands' to point up what war has done to landscape.[17]

Blunden, a shepherd in war, is distinctly sharp-eyed, and very aware of corruption in Arcadia. *Undertones of War* uses an epigraph from John Bunyan and the text (p. 7) speaks of 'the ebony walking-stick which had been my grandfather's, and was to be my pilgrim's staff'. The prose text has 'A Supplement of poetical interpretations and variations', which suggests a continuum between prose and verse. An important part of Blunden's prose, however, is detachment, in the sense that he presents a figure who is passing through a landscape of experience. A desire to survive is strong, and the survival needs to be psychological as much as physical. This does not call for coldness (Blunden feels strongly for people and things) but it does mean that the satirical element in his verse seems designed to keep a distance on the horrors. An irony that records satirical contrasts works in these poems to keep the individual sane. The war is 'senseless rage': the sensible person observes this and so avoids the blindness of the Grenfell-warrior. But awareness of this rage does not lead, with Blunden, to the assault on Home which Sassoon mounts. It is as if, for Blunden, it would be enough for the guns to stop firing and the landscape begin to recover. A curious poem called 'Premature Rejoicing' makes the point.[18] In it Titania, in Thiepval

Wood, scene of terrible fighting, 'Looks ahead ten years/And sees
her Wood again, and her usual Grenadiers,/All in green'. That time
is in the future, of course, and, for the moment, there is 'difficulty' –
the war. If Sassoon's war poems should inhibit war-making by
communicating the cost in ruined lives, Blunden's fold that cost into
the wider context of buildings, land and history. But neither poet
offers much by way of analysis. Sassoon, as we have seen, projects
fantasies of bombers clearing Parliament; Blunden became
indentified with Fascism.

Satire did not provide a way of understanding the war, except on a
local level, although it might be more accurate to say that no poet of
the war found a way of deploying satire to answer the questions
engendered by it. But, as with Blunden, satire can help preserve
poise and sanity. Similarly, poise can seem satirical, even where
intention is unclear, as in Maud Bell's poem 'From a Trench'.[19] Bell
works by contrast, between 'spoilt and battered fields' with grass
trampled 'Into a purple slime' and 'crocuses at Nottingham':

> There are crocuses at Nottingham!
> Wild crocuses at Nottingham!
> Blue crocuses at Nottingham!
> Though here the grass is red.

At Nottingham there is also innocence about the war; innocence
which extends to folly: 'There are silly fools at Nottingham/Who
think we're here for fun'. The truth is that 'There are crocuses at
Nottingham! . . . Because we're here in Hell'. The poem intimates
unknowingness at Home, and the shift from innocence to folly puts
pressure on those who struggle in hell. It may be admirable to
defend innocence, but is it more than folly to defend folly? The gap
Bell's poem articulates carries two-way satirical implications, but her
poem, unsettling though it is, marks out a gap while formulating no
closure.

Such marking of gaps is the most common function of the verse
satire of the war, and it constitutes a critique of idealism, obviously
enough. Blunden's guard, flustered into resuming his role of 'terror
of the Hun', would rather (sanely) yield to the appeal of pastoral.
Ford Madox Ford's 'That Exploit of Yours'[20] deflates the idea of
glorious military deeds and the concept of patriotic duty, while Ivor
Gurney undercuts doctrines of unquestioning obedience in 'The
Silent One':

> The politest voice – a finicking accent, said:

> 'Do you think you might crawl through there: there's a hole'.
> Darkness, shot at: I smiled, as politely replied –
> 'I'm afraid not, Sir'. . . .[21]

Edgell Rickword presents the soldier as concerned with survival, through an address by the soldier to his body:

> I shall be mad if you get smashed about,
> We've had good times together, you and I. . . .

And the point of surviving is to have more good times, exploring the 'world of things we've never done',[22] this being the world of the senses. Heroism is out, both now and in the future.

There is clearly disillusionment in such satirical poems about conditions at the Front, and this may be seen in context of the running fire of undercutting irony in such trench newspapers as *The Wipers Times*. The irony of these papers, however, is of the order of comic grumbling. Implications are often subversive, but the impression is of acceptance, with the grumbling as a safety-valve. So far as I know, authority made no effort to suppress the trench newspapers. Similarly, the effect of the satirical poetry about trench experience is too localised and particular to present much of a challenge to the war. Sassoon is a partial exception, but is largely isolated, contained by the way the army treated him, as a neurasthenic hero. Success for satire from the trenches, in the sense of changing policy and/or stopping the war, could only have come through incitement to action, but British mutinies are very largely confined to the end of the war. We have already noticed that satire has failed to prevent war's recurrence.

Sassoon directed his satire at Home, and he was far from being the only poet to point to Home failure to understand what was happening at the Front. But satire of Home tends, like satire of conditions at the Front, to be particular and to observe rather than to analyse. One of Sassoon's particularities involves bitter hostility to women. With females barred from the fighting itself, they were confined to various support roles. They might, as nurses, come close to the fighting and very close to its effects, and many women worked in munitions factories, furthering the war effort by maintaining the supply of arms. Women 'have helped the cause' also by providing goods and clothing for serving armies and, of course, by endorsing recruitment drives and pro-war propaganda. Finally, they offered both licit and illicit sexual services.

It follows that women who wrote poems about the war could adopt any of a number of postures. Brookean themes could be used and a lot of patriotic verse was written by women, as well as poems to help recruitment and to indicate female support for the efforts being made by men actually involved in the fighting. But women poets, by virtue of being barred from direct military activity and from the politics bearing on it, had the opportunity to dissociate themselves from the making of the war and its perpetuation. One possible version of this would be satire, and a number of women poets of the war used the mode.

Women were particularly well-placed to observe the returning soldier. Sassoon reads this as part of the obscenity of Home, seeing women as sustaining myths about the war and getting sexual thrills from tales of dirt and danger. Alternatively, they simply fail, in his eyes, to understand what war experience is; and so the woman of 'Supreme Sacrifice' has eyes which suggest 'she'd felt the shock/Of ugly war brought home', but 'then a slow/Spiritual brightness stole across her face' and she comments that ' "*they* are safe and happy now" ', eliciting the sour thought ' "The world's a silly sort of place/When people think it's pleasant to be dead" '.[23] But Sassoon is less than fair, for women were more sensitive than he suggests. Vera Brittain, who lost a brother and her fiancé, has a bitter 'Lament of the Demobilised' which registers the disgust of those who returned to discover that others had 'stayed behind and just got on', and that 'no one talked heroics now'.[24] To have gone to fight is now seen as folly. Margaret Postgate Cole writes in 1916 of a veteran 'Blinded by war' who, says the last line, is 'Nineteen, the third of May'. Such anecdote poems articulate sympathy and obviously distance the writers from unthinking chauvinism or vicarious thrills; and the sense of distancing occurs in a few poems by women which attack aspects of their own sex. So May O'Rourke is contemptuous of those who, with 'darkened lashes' and 'scented hands', forget the dead 'who went to die/To save her light blue eyes from dreadful scenes' – but her poem is carefully called 'The Minority'. Helen Hamilton attacks 'Jingo-woman' for stupid complacency, her exasperation coming through the technical bareness of her style: 'Oh! exasperating woman,/I'd like to wring your neck,/I really would!/You make all women seem such duffers!'. She comes closer to Sassoon with 'The Ghouls', figures who 'gloat with dulled old eyes' over casualty lists, drawing 'Fresh life/New value 'from' their young bodies'.

Gertrude Ford, however, suggests an alignment of women with the dying, the poor, the wounded, and with Christ, against the war-lords, the profiteers, the 'Jingo-kind', the 'Armament-kings', hate, and the church. The poem, 'A Fight to a Finish', suggests that the views of women, aligned as suggested above, are ignored by the forces that want the war to go on:

> Nobody asked what the women thought.[25]

Moreover, the inclusion of 'the poor in the starveling years' makes the attack on supporters of the war partly a social attack, while Christ here is the deity of the underprivileged. The poor, women and the actual combatants have, it is suggested, a common cause; and what is adumbrated is a broader revolution than Sassoon's *putsch* by the returning military.

Women seem more likely to use satire than male non-combatants, and to use it to question aspects of the war. G.K. Chesterton becomes satirical on behalf of the Unknown Soldier, but does so because – as a result of publicity (a false version of honour and praise) – the war must be seen in terms of 'ignoble days'. 'The one great pleasure' is 'Fame without name and glory without gossip', while the poem shows its patriotism through its anti-Americanism.[26] Chesterton is questioning an aspect of how the war was received, as is D.S. MacColl with his squib about striking miners (1915):

> The present desperate stage
> Of fighting brings us luck;
> And in the higher war we wage
> (For higher wage) *We struck*.[27]

But male non-combatant satire is rare: scarcely visible among the eulogies, although Hardy, Kipling and Houseman come close at times to satirical attitudes.

What remains is a number of poems which are best seen as working close to aspects of Sassoon's satire. Julian Grenfell's 'Prayer for those on the Staff',[28] when taken with his more famous 'Into Battle', makes the point that excited acceptance of the war is not incompatible with satirising a particular feature of it, but Grenfell's satire is genial, whereas A.P. Herbert, in 'After the Battle', insinu-ates both weariness and bitterness:

> You will come up in your capacious car
> To find your heroes sulking in the rain,

> To tell us how magnificent we are,
> And how you hope we'll do the same again.[29]

'We . . . have bled to boost you up a rung' and are left to 'mourn those spaces in the mess'. So the poem ends with a blank acceptance of division between Front and Staff:

> Fight, if you must, fresh battles far ahead,
> But keep them dark behind your chateau door!

Osbert Sitwell attacks older generations and profiteers, but his satire is blurred by comparison with Sassoon's, while anti-Semitism is unpleasantly prominent.

E.A. Mackintosh's 'Recruiting' is, in context, an important poem.[30] Mackintosh joined the Seaforth Highlanders in 1914, was in France the following year, won the Military Cross, was gassed and wounded on the Somme and killed at Cambrai. His poems manage to combine a lack of illusion with assurance about the value of what he is doing. 'Recruiting' rewrites its title, being a satire on those who produced the propaganda of recruitment, especially that of the early months of the war. Those who 'penned the call' ('Lads, you're wanted, go and help') include 'Fat civilians' exempt through age and 'Girls with feathers'. The honest message would be

> 'Lads, you're wanted! over there',
> Shiver in the morning dew,
> More poor devils like yourselves
> Waiting to be killed by you.

The real impulse of the recruiters is to get recruits 'to keep them nice and safe/From the wicked German foe'. But Mackintosh goes on to substitute an appeal which marks total alienation from the Home of 'blasted journalists', harlots singing comic songs about the Hun and 'fat old men' who demand vicarious participation ('Now *we've* got them on the run'). The new appeal is

>     Come and learn
> To live and die with honest men. . .
> . . . . . . . . . .
> Learn the gaiety and strength
> In the gallant sacrifice. . .
> . . . . . . . . . .
> Live clean or go out quick –
> Lads, you're wanted. Come and die.

Ideas of Brookean patriotism have been relocated. War is a cleansing, can be gay and gallant – but only if Home is rejected. Moreover, there is no suggestion of a collective attack on Home along the lines of Sassoon's bombers. The learning is self-valuing and will, it seems, end in death.

But perhaps the most extreme satirical poem of the war was written by A.G. West, killed in his mid-twenties in April 1917, having, it seems, become a pacifist before a sniper got him. His 'God, how I hate you, you young cheerful men' uses powerful, ugly detail in Sassoon's manner:

> his head
> Smashed like an egg-shell, and the warm grey brain
> Spattered all bloody on the parados. . . .[31]

This detail puts extreme pressure on poets who speak of 'these epic days' ('And *he'd* been to France'), on religious optimism ('Yet still God's in His Heaven, all is right/In the best possible of worlds') and on the idea of a God who is 'A genial umpire, a good judge of sport'. The idea of the war as something which prevents the rusting of youthfulness is also attacked, and in this poem the Christ who seems 'to walk/The bloody fields of Flanders' has come to resemble Moloch. West's poem is an extreme revisionist summary: ideal upon ideal is undercut, without any of the dignity which Mackintosh expressed. Moreover, West's cry of hatred goes nowhere. There is no collectivism, neither Sassoon's nor Gertrude Ford's.

Satire is often seen by satirists as sanative, working by physic or surgery to restore health to the body (social, national, individual) which it is administered to. Often, the satirical poetry of the First World War seems a response which may keep the satirist sane. Where satire enters the work of T.B. Clark it helps him sustain the role of 'Tommy', while for Blunden it makes room for the shepherd to believe that history will be restored when the fighting stops. Satire gives Sassoon something to live for (revenge) and it allows several women writers to claim solidarity with the suffering. It questions the war by raising issues of cost, profit and loss, insisting that the price may be too high. In this sense, most of this satire is anti-war, but it is more accurate to say that it is against the conduct, prolongation and conditions of *this* war. Little of it could accurately be called pacifist and most of it has its roots in the particular circumstances of the First World War itself. There were few satirical poems questioning the war at its outset: the satirists were working at propaganda against Germans, pacifists and other 'shirkers'. Obviously, it could be argued that protest arising from the specific conditions of this war can have validity for war in general, since war is always disgusting and brutal. Sadly, however, it seems that protest is not enough. Although the (usually quite brief) satirical poems of the war tend to cohere around alienation from the conditions the combatants endured and a sense that the real enemies were Staff and Home, this degree of consistency cannot convincingly be seen either as an attack on war in general or as an attack on the First World War in the name of any set of social, political or religious beliefs, or with an analysis and programme which might have ended war with the ending of the First World War. This is not to denigrate the poets discussed in this chapter, but to indicate how limited satire's efficacy is, if it is as isolated as in this war. And perhaps no more could reasonably have been hoped for than what was achieved. Liberalism and international socialism both collaborated with the war, as did the bulk of the suffragette movement; the conservatives were always likely to do so and the establishment church was too implicated in Empire to protest very much. As for individuals, the courage of Sassoon's protest is only matched by the shallowness of his socialism, while the isolationism of the public schools made deep contact with the underprivileged unlikely. The satirical tendencies of the underprivileged themselves were isolated and contained: cheerful grumbling by 'Tommy' and a tentative search for solidarity by some women.

## NOTES

1. In *The Supreme Sacrifice*, Skeffington, 1919, p. 36.
2. Haste, p. 3.
3. *The Collected Poems, with a Memoir by Edward Marsh*, Sidgwick and Jackson, 1918.
4. Delany, p. 151ff.
5. Ed. J.A. Hammerton, n.d.
6. Dobell, 1915.
7. 'The Modern Machiavellians', 'Germany's Oracles', 'The Destruction of Louvain'.
8. *The Unutterable Beauty*, Hodder and Stoughton, 16th ed. n.d. p. 44.
9. 'Belgium Held the Way to the Battlefield', Tulloch, p. 35.
10. Tulloch, p. 39.

11. Hussey, p. 152.
12. Tulloch, pp. 146, 150, 154.
13. *The War Poems*, p. 15. All the quotations below are from this volume.
14. *Poems of a Private*, Nicholson, n.d.
15. (1928), Penguin, 1936.
16. Parsons, p. 118.
17. *Undertones of War*, pp. 271, 252, 250, 258.
18. Hibberd/Onions, p. 108.
19. Catherine Reilly, *Scars upon my Heart*, Virago, 1981, pp. 10–11.
20. *The Penguin Book of First World War Poetry*, ed. J. Silkin, Penguin, 1979, p. 141.
21. *Collected Poems*, ed. P.J. Kavanagh, Oxford, 1982, p. 102.
22. 'The Soldier Addresses his Body', Silkin, p. 133.
23. *War Poems*, p. 81.
24. Reilly, p. 14.
25. ibid. pp. 22, 86, 47, 38.
26. 'To the Unknown Warrior', Parsons, ed. *Men who March Away*, Chatto and Windus, 1965, p. 89.
27. 'The Miners' Response', Gardner, p.75.
28. E. Black, ed., *1914–18 in Poetry*, Hodder and Stoughton, 1970, p. 102.
29. Gardner, p. 121.
30. ibid. p. 111.
31. Hibberd/Onions, p. 158.

# 4

# THE VOICE OF THE NON-COMMISSIONED

Since so much of the verse of the First World War was written by officers it may seem strange to devote a complete chapter to the issue of non-commissioned voices. But privates made up the vast majority of the armies of the war. The phenomenon of huge British armies is the phenomenon of the ranker. It is *because* so much of the verse of the war is of genteel authorship that we should be alive to the possibility of its misrepresenting the reactions of the ordinary soldier and consider the issue of such soldiers' voices.

But, on the way to this topic, there are clichés to negotiate: the idea of the 'poor bloody infantry' and that of 'Tommy', with his cheerful endurance (epitomised in the most popular examples of Bairnsfather's work). There is the cliché of cheerful 'cockney' grumbling about mud and rations (T.B. Clark). There is also elision to be taken into account (those many poems in which the protagonist is simply a soldier, of no given rank), together with the perennial genteel tendency to generalise the non-genteel into the mass of the working class. Then there is the cultural pressure for the less privileged to play up to the roles defined for them by the privileged and there is the problem that unequivocally authentic voices of the non-commissioned (whatever these may be) are rarely heard.

I mean by this last point that, relative to the millions of ordinary people who served in the war or who were related to such participants, very few have left any record that survives. Letters and diaries do exist, some preserved in print and others in manuscript, much of the latter material precariously in family homes. Some reminiscences have now been taped – interviews with survivors of 1914–18 – and there are extant poems. The total bulk (so far as this is ascertainable) allows for some tentative conclusions, but this bulk is minute when compared with the complete, mass experience. Moreover, it is impossible to say how typical what survives may be, simply because survival itself gives cause for suspicion if we are looking for the typical; and this is perhaps where we should begin.

It has been said that the British armies of the First World War were the first to be fully literate, and the suggestion of national literacy here could be taken to indicate that almost everyone might become a poet of the war. Eric Hobsbawm speaks of the late nineteenth century as the age of primary education;[1] Donald Read remarks that, by around 1850, 66 to 75 per cent 'of the English working class could probably read at least passably well';[2] Lawson and Silver refer to almost 2,500 schools boards being established in England and Wales following the 1870 Elementary Education Act. It seems that literacy increased by nearly 20 per cent for males and almost 25 per cent for females in the thirty years to 1900, with – as we might expect – the main advance being among the 'most depressed classes'.[3] Thompson says that *Lloyds Weekly News* was selling a million copies in the 1890s, while the *Daily Mail* was close to that figure in 1900[4] and the *Mirror* exceeded it in 1912. The nineteenth century saw the rise of cheap commercial publishing, the Public Libraries Act of 1850, the rise of circulating libraries like Smith's and Mudie's, developments in adult education and (mainly towards the century's end) in university provision.

Reading, at any level, is a complex matter, and the mechanics of writing can be mastered independently of the acquisition of reading skills. But written composition is another matter, involving externalisation of what you know and the rendering of this as another person's reading material. It would be sentimental to believe that a child leaving a board school in 1900 at the age of 14 was equipped to write anything very demanding. It is to the point that this is the great period of *primary* education: responding in writing to the war called for more than such education could provide.

It is intrinsically likely, therefore, that relatively few people involved in the war in any capacity had a developed ability to write about their experiences, at least in an orthodoxly sustained or creative way. The provision of standardised cards for the troops to send home can be seen not only as a form of censorship, but also as a recognition of the helplessness of many faced with the need to communicate in writing. John Laffin has claimed that 'The rank and file were . . . ill-educated and often only functionally literate', and, in his anthology, quotes a model letter written by an officer in the manner of 'the men'.[5] This is clearly dangerous evidence, and even as a parody shows more than functional literacy; while Dr Ron Chand, a linguistician, tells me that the diaries of rankers which he has examined are thoroughly competent. Yet diary-keeping was discouraged in the British Army and I know of no evidence that it was at all common among products of mass elementary education. Like a memoir such as George Coppard's,[6] the quality of surviving diaries is likely to mark the writer as exception rather than norm.

Verse, of course, is a highly organised form of writing. As song it may be both popular and a product of mass-composition, but it is usually the construct of a small minority. Few non-genteel people can have left school with much experience of writing verse (as distinct from copying or memorising the compositions of others). It is perhaps surprising that the 'masses' gave back anything other than a resounding silence.

Yet there is no lack of claims to speak for the inarticulate, or, more accurately, no lack of voices which, theoretically, might prove authentic. Superficially, at least, the most plausible will be verses written by non-officers and the adaptations of songs and hymns which survive. But in what sense can a non-officer be *representative* of the 'masses'? How far can a collectively-composed adaptation of a song or hymn reveal the inner life of an individual? Then there are officer-poets who, like Sassoon and Owen, come to see their task as to speak for the 'poor bloody infantry'. Such poets sometimes try to represent the speech of the ranker as dialect. Yet how far can an officer speak for a ranker? There are also ranker-poets of genteel background. How representative can they be?

I shall concentrate upon four varieties of representation, all of which are products of direct experience of the war. A brief look at what I have called elision will be followed by a short discussion of the poetry of men who served as rankers, although not themselves of 'ranker class'. There are, thirdly, several poets who seem to be 'genuine' rankers and, finally, three special cases: W.W. Gibson, Isaac Rosenberg and Ivor Gurney.

Just before his death, Wilfred Owen, in a letter to his mother, wrote famously about what he had come to see as his primary poetic function:

> I came out in order to help these boys – directly by leading them as well as an officer can; indirectly, by watching their sufferings that I may

speak of them as well as a pleader can.[7]

Clearly, Owen is not here claiming that he can be the authentic voice of 'these boys' – and that phrase is itself revealing. As an officer he helps by leading and as a poet by 'pleading' their cause/case as well as he can. The passage marks sympathetic division rather than elision of differences, yet Owen's poetry mediates between these extremes. He has a few poems, like 'The Letter', which purport to be by a Cockney soldier, who is, it seems, no officer; and there are others ('The Dead-Beat') which register the division between officer and soldier, while making it clear that the officer-poet sympathises with the ranker. But such poems as 'Dulce et Decorum est' and 'Asleep' blur the distinction and the voices of 'The Last Laugh' might be those of either officers or troops. In 'Exposure' the plural pronouns provide a collective identity. Similarly, Sassoon's 'Counter-attack' has a collective we. This poem also uses a 'he' ('A yawning soldier') who is perhaps a private, but what is important is that this 'he' represents the group undertaking the counter-attack, while the poem's specified officer is only a transient.

I do not mean to suggest here that officer-poets forgot that, in rank and culture, they were usually unlike the men they led. But their main concern when they seem to ignore the differences is to convey the collective experience of groups sharing the pressures of the war – or what they deem this experience to be. It is significant that when Owen tries to speak with the tongue of the ranker, as in 'The Letter', he can do no better than stage-Cockney. When, in 'Inspection', he has a ranker reflect on being disciplined for being 'dirty on parade', the reference to 'the damned spot' (*Macbeth*) can be taken as the officer's literary version of the soldier's reaction to his blood being seen as dirt, but when the soldier comments

'The world is washing out its stains' . . .
'It doesn't like our cheeks so red:
Young blood's its great objection. . . .'

a reader must either assume a poetic soldier or a refined version of ranker-language. In the letter quoted from above, Owen writes of watching the suffering of 'these boys'. Suffering can be shared, but this does not mean that Owen can tell us how a non-privileged ranker felt about it. When he tries (as 'The Chances'), the result is embarrassing in the awkwardness of the attempt at someone else's language:

An'one, to use the word of 'ypocrites,
'Ad the misfortoon to be took be Fritz.

When officers like Owen and Sassoon speak of wanting to write on behalf of 'these boys', they are perhaps suggesting that the men in question cannot write for themselves; and we have seen that this was probably true. The desire to 'plead' also indicates appreciation of the troops: they deserve a pleader, and one is perhaps reminded of how badly the minority of deserters fared when lacking adequate voices and responsive ears. We might expect the few genteel males who served in the ranks to go further than officers in identifying and representing the reactions of the ordinary soldier – but they do not.

There are two chief examples in English prose fiction of the war of presenting that war from a ranker-perspective. One is Henry Williamson's *Private's Progress*, in which the protagonist is allegorised, and the other is Frederic Manning's *Her Private We*. In Manning's novel the protagonist, Bourne, is a ranker of officer-class who resists attempts to persuade him to seek a commission. Bourne remains a separate figure, however, cut off culturally from other soldiers, while segregated by military rank from his officers. His peculiar position is valuable but necessarily idiosyncratic. Something similar is true of a small group of poets who served in the ranks but who were culturally officer-class.

Wilfrid Halliday, for example, went to war with an MA from the University of Leeds but enlisted as a private in 1914. He was a second lieutenant by 1917 and his poem 'An Unknown British Soldier' seems to belong to the period after his commissioning.[8] It is a decent 'pleading' for the unknown soldier, but it conveys no sense either of a putatively distinct ranker-response or that its poet's experience as a ranker has shaped a response of any individuality. Alexander Robertson, a corporal in the York and Lancaster Regiment, went missing in July 1916 and was presumably killed in action. Internal evidence suggests that he was educated at Oxford: his few poems could quite easily be those of an officer. A.G. West is more interesting.

West was educated at Blundell's and Oxford, and applied for a commission in 1914. He was rejected because of defective eyesight, but joined the ranks of the Public Schools Battalion in February 1915. He served in France as a ranker between November 1915 and March 1916; was finally commissioned in September 1916, only to be killed in April 1917. The Public Schools Battalion could hardly

have given West much contact with the perspectives of the ordinary
soldier and his eventual pacifism suggests a more developed hostility
to the war than most soldiers articulated. 'God, how I Hate You'
(discussed earlier) is an example of the erosion of officer and ranker
into a single figure, while 'The Night Patrol' works along similar
lines.[9] In the latter poem the voice which gives instructions at the
beginning must be that of an officer. The three soldiers who conduct
the patrol, however, might include a junior officer or an NCO (or
both). They are unlikely to be three rankers, but the important
points are that they are collectively seen and that the defining terms
of the 'I' who is one of the party are genteel: although 'we' take
notice of the attitudes of corpses as guides to the route back from the
patrol, it is 'I' who smiled at a particular corpse 'that lay on his back
and crossed/His legs Crusader-wise', and 'thought on Elia and his
Temple Church'. The overall voice of the poem is of someone with
literary experience and, more broadly, of considerable practice in
writing. West's poems, in fact, operate with much the same terms as
those of Owen and Sassoon.

Another interesting figure is Leslie Coulson, a journalist before
the war who, having refused a commission, became a platoon
sergeant. He joined the Royal Fusiliers in September 1914, served in
Egypt and Malta, was wounded at Gallipoli and killed on the Somme
in 1916. His volume, *From an Outpost* (1917), is said to have sold
10,000 copies in a year. Coulson's work is mostly orthodox literary
verse, giving no specific sense of a non-officer voice:

> One little hour, – how short it is
>   When Love with dew-eyed loveliness
> Raises her lips for ours to kiss
>   And dies within our first caress
>                             ('. . . But a Short Time to Live')[10]

He seems concerned to transform actualities into myths. So the
tavern of 'From the Somme' is nostalgically improbable:

> Oft in the tavern parlour I would sing
>   Of morning sun upon the mountain vine
> And, calling for a chorus, sweep the string
>   In praise of good red wine.[11]

In 'The God who Waits' industrial England is represented by 'marts
and mills', and the desired post-war location is elswhere:

> For still beyond the city gate,

The fallow fields eternal wait
For us to drive our future straight.[12]

Coulson is far from incompetent, and a poem written about two months before his death, 'The Rainbow', has both restrained reality of location and some real tension:

> Blood at night is red,
> Yea, even at night,
> And a dead man's face is white.
> And I dry my hands, that are also trained to kill,
> And I look at the stars – for the stars are beautiful still.[13]

But what is interesting in Coulson is that, working with stock themes and images, he is sometimes able to animate them, by detail or by the twist at the end of his sonnet, 'Judgment':

> Then shall my soul soar up and summon Thee
> To tell me *why*. And as Thou answerest,
> So shall I judge Thee, God, not Thou judge me.[14]

This rebellion could be the product of service as an NCO, but it could as easily be the voice of an officer.

It seems obvious that poets who are of 'ranker-class' would be more likely to be able to express the perceptions and responses of those who had no more than the basic education thought appropriate for the 'masses'; but two factors should give us pause before we take their poems at face value. First, the very fact of being able to produce poems argues for a level of literacy beyond the norm of the early twentieth century (or later), while the evidence of lowly-born poets like Stephen Duck and John Clare indicates that they are likely to be under pressure from the elite who usually control publishing to conform to their expectations of acceptable style. The ranker poets I have come across were, it appears, usually unable to resist such pressure.

T.B. Clark was looked at in an earlier chapter. His *Poems of a Private* gives the impression of a professional soldier who is proud of his army and regiment, has a sense of an idealised military past, and who is content to play the part of the 'cheerful Cockney'. Clark has, it seems, quite a firm grasp of idiom, uses his verse forms confidently and does include details of army life at the private's level. But there is little in his volume to suggest an inner life; little that feels particular rather than shaped for Home consumption of a finally reassuring sort. It remains possible, of course, that Clark's military experience had atrophied his inner life (rather as C.S. Forester's general is a husk). This is, however, a distinctly unpleasant thought.

Patrick MacGill was an Irishman who seems to have been navvy, tramp and journalist before the war. He joined the London Irish Rifles, was wounded at Loos, and became a sergeant. His *Soldier Songs* (1916) was published by Herbert Jenkins and, as a physical object, is superior to Clark's. The dedication (to H.J., presumably Jenkins) discusses 'what are the favourite songs of the soldier, the rhymed lines which give expression to his soul'. He says that 'The soldiers have songs of their own, songs of the march, the trench, the billet and battle. Their origin is lost; the songs have arisen like old folk-tales', but he adds that 'Most of the verse is of no import; the crowd has no sense of poetic values; it is the singing alone which gives expression to the soldier's soul'. MacGill gives a few examples, including the fine chorus to 'Sing me to Sleep':

> Far, far from Ypres I long to be,
> Where German snipers can't get at me,
> Think of me crouching where the worms creep,
> Waiting for the sergeant to sing me to sleep.[15]

MacGill argues, finally, that these songs will not outlive the war.

There is both affection and deprecation here; but also a sense of separation. MacGill knows about 'poetic values', it would seem. He may well be right about the origins of soldier songs and usefully points to them as a 'mystery'. Further, the idea that the value is in the singing is plausible enough: finding your voice in the collective effort of the scarcely-educated. But MacGill's own poems are called 'Soldier Songs', although he neither explicitly links them with the songs his dedication discusses nor (like Clark) suggests that they represent a generalised view of 'Tommy'. The poems, however, look like efforts at what Home expects, in which things are sanitised and rhythms are persistently cheery:

> And when we took the cobbled road
>     We often took before,
> Our thoughts were with the hearty lads
>     Who trod that way no more.
> Oh! lads out on the level fields,
>     If you could call to mind
> The good red wine of Nouex-les-Mines

You would not stay behind!

('Red Wine')

MacGill uses slang which is explained in footnotes ('blighty blue', 'Daisy-shovers' – both in 'The Ole Sweats') and has several poems in cockneyese. The latter seldom look really convincing in print, but they conform to the Home convention that 'cockney' is what rankers speak when not using standard English. MacGill is a perfectly competent user of standard (at least on the evidence of the printed text) and a capable creator of slightly generalised effects:

> In the fields between the trenches are a million blossoms
> springing
> 'Twixt the grass of silver bayonets where the lines of
> battle wind
> Where man has manned the trenches for the maiming of his
> kind.

('The Trench')

When I bought my second-hand copy of *Soldier Songs* it had two newspaper clippings in it. One contains a report of a talk MacGill seems to have given somewhere about his verse-writing before the war, while the other, from the *Newcastle Chronicle*, is headed 'Navvy Poet from Old Donegal', and is a summary of another MacGill talk about his life, at least up to the time of the war. This cutting speaks of MacGill having 'a brogue as rich as it must have been when he left . . . the wild coast of Donegal some twenty years ago', and it ends with a brief quotation in which the poet claims 'The Great Unwashed – of them I sing'. Unfortunately, the brogue is written out of *Soldier Songs* and the unwashed have been cleansed. MacGill is an interesting poet of the war, but he does not convince as a ranker-voice, except in the sense that he was a ranker and found a voice.

Much the same is true of Joseph Lee, who was an NCO in the Black Watch and who served in France and Flanders. Murray published his *Ballads of Battle* in 1916 and *Work-a-day Warriors* the following year. Osborn includes four of his poems in *The Muse in Arms* and he was printed in such journals as *The Spectator* and *The Nation*. Like MacGill, Lee is a competent writer of verse, handling well-established lyric and ballad forms with assurance; and, like Clark, he has a sense of his poems as speaking for 'Tommy'. So 'Nocturnals' is sub-titled 'Tommy's Night Thoughts in the Trenches' and uses dialect. But the dialect is modfied Scots:

> O, I wad gi'e a hell o'a lot
>     For the sight o'a Scottish hill,
>         For the clasp o'a Scottish lassie's waist,
>         And - weel - just to say a little taste
>     O'a guid auld Scottish gill!

Yet in 'Pick and Spade' ('The plaint of Tommy - aching') dialect is uneasily divided between Scots and cockney. Elsewhere, Lee writes standard:

> And when they found him at the dawn,
>     His brow with blood defiled,
> And gently laid him in the earth,
>     They wondered that he smiled.

('The Mother')

Occasional instructive footnotes suggest that Lee felt anxious to interpret aspects of Tommy-experience to a Home audience, and (despite intermittent grumbling of Clark's kind) the presentation is basically heartening, with the cheery confidence of

> And when the war is over -
>     The war we mean to win -
>     And Kaiser Bill
>     Has had his pill,
> And we boys march thro' Berlin

('The Mouth-Organ')

Lee's volumes mix poems and drawings (by the author) in a way which defines a war effort that draws in Gurkhas and Sikhs (Empire) as well as the French (Allies); and this effort is seen as involving a superiority to Home:

> The men who stay at home at ease
> Need never try to wash their knees
> In dixie lids - yet never fear,
> I'd rather far be dirty here!

(' "Stay-at-home Hearts are Best" ')[16]

Lee's drawings are assured, but in a comforting idiom. Even 'Via Dolorosa', which shows Italians carrying a wounded soldier from the trenches, is dignified, while 'Ruined Church at Elverdinghe' seems more Romantic than ravaged.[17]

These two volumes have considerable range, and the experiences they are concerned with are consistently seen from ranker-perspectives. His use of language, centred on his command of standard, extends beyond Scots and cockney to a version of Canadian ('War')

and Irish ('St Patrick's Day in the Mornin' '), and this – taken with
the drawings – indicates community, the point being made by the
modifications of dialect to ease communication. Moreover, Lee's war
is continuous with the past, in his use of relatively popular traditional forms, in his cultural allusions, and in his handling of history. In
the final resort, the detail Lee uses in some poems and the rehearsals
of set-pieces of war experience (like 'Sick Parade') are sublimated to
the 'universality' of a lyric like 'The Willow Tree':

> We soldiers who are sleeping
>   Until the Day of Doom?
> O, Willow, Willow weeping,
> So soundly are we sleeping.[18]

Lee's sincerity is not in question, but his volumes seem tailored to
Home and a sense of public duty. They are conducive to keeping up
morale, both at the front and at home. The poems are neither
complacent nor crudely propagandist, and they are free of hatred,
but they lack a sense of personality. There is 'A Shakespeare
Tercentenary in the Trenches',[19] which begins:

> Three centuries agone since Shakespeare died,
> Since he was shrouded in good English ground . . . .

The poet imagines reading Shakespeare at the Front:

> And here sit I, a tattered Corporal,
> Reading me snatches from a tattered tome,
> In fateful Flanders in a fetid trench,
> While round me lie six lads in ravelled hose,
> Torn kilts, and broken shoon, and lousy shirts,
> Like his own Falstaff's ragged regiment.

The meditation which follows is informed and quite detailed, but
Shakespeare remains a reassuring national icon:

> And yet, and yet, if only England live
> Our life is but a little thing to give.

The analysis does not go inwards to create any sense of a particular
psyche responding to what is being experienced.

Neither Lee nor MacGill is untalented, and both are clearly more
than functionally literate. Yet the literacy which makes them
exceptional among rankers operates to make their poems unconvinc-
ing as accounts of ranker experience. Neither produces anything
which records the physical squalor in Sassoon's detail and neither

has, nor creates, an idiom which is convincing as a ranker-voice, either in language or in form. It seems as if such poets can only draw on traditions not their own. MacGill's deprecation of soldiers' songs is significant here: they are not Art, and MacGill is pressed to produce Art. It should, however, be added that the type of poetry they wrote is highly revealing, in various ways. The absence of detailed accounts of squalor may indicate that for a Lee or a MacGill trench conditions seemed less appalling than for public school officers, or it may indicate sensitivity about what should be drawn to Home attention. The lack of a sense of individuality may say something about how the war denied individuality, while the same lack suggests that the decay of popular culture was far advanced by 1914. Osborn, reflecting in the introduction to *Muse in Arms* upon the lack of dialect poems, sees music hall and the 'strange, literary convention . . . of Cockneyese' as 'malign' influences which prevent the possibility of this war providing 'a few English marching-songs equal in power and freshness' to those of the American Civil War. He comforts himself, however, with the observation that the forces no longer speak 'Cockney', for 'to-day . . . generally speaking, the King's fighting men – an educated nation in arms . . . speak the King's English'.[20] It is an astonishing statement in several ways, but, when referred to how people might write, it does point to the heart of the issue. It is true that most efforts at dialect in poetry of the war are 'Cockney', and it is equally true that war poets work hard at writing 'King's English' (though who gave our language to the monarchy I do not know). When the deprecation of music hall is linked with MacGill's deprecation of the songs of the soldiers, there is a picture which seems to reduce the chances of a convincing ranker-voice almost to zero.

The idea of a genuine dialect poetry of the war is, sadly, a non-starter: here Osborn is basically right. The most intriguing possibility of an exception lies with D.H. Lawrence, who wrote some impressive Nottinghamshire dialect poems in the early years of the century. But Lawrence, of course, was opposed to serving in the forces and was rejected for military service when conscription came in. But he writes war poems – in standard English. Elsewhere, there is largely 'Cockney' and almost always either incompetence in rendering dialect or an uneasy felt need to dilute for the imagined audience. The few poets who, I think, do render something that feels convincingly like an individual ranker-voice manage this largely without recourse to dialect.

A rather surprising case is that of W.W. Gibson. Gibson became a ranker in the RASC after being rejected for service four times. Hibberd and Onions say that he was never abroad,[21] and Gibson is nobody's idea of an untutored voice. He was a friend of such as Brooke, Sassoon and Abercrombie; appears in the *Georgian Poetry* anthologies; and had published several small volumes by 1914. His main volume of war poems, *Battle*, came out in 1915, before he had been accepted for service. Yet Gibson does at times find a manner which comes over as a convincing version of non-privileged experience: when he does this it is a case of the plain modesty of the best Georgian verse paying off.

Gibson's voices are not necessarily those of non-officers, but where rank and social standing are indicated the suggestions are of the ordinary soldier. The voice of 'Mangel-Wurzels' remembers 'Hoeing for the squire,/Down in Gloucestershire'; the parent of 'Nightmare' recalls a son who has 'taken the king's shilling' (which officers did not do); and the memories of 'The Reek' are of peat-fires and ingle-seats. Gibson is also able to use dialect within the context of standard English ('syke' in 'Deaf'; 'Gey' and 'bumming' in 'The Question') but he seems unconcerned with full-scale renderings of dialect speech, doing just enough, where appropriate, to indicate deviance. It would not be accurate to claim that Gibson gives any strong sense of individual responses to the war, but he does have a feeling for the ordinary and is not in the business of creating 'Tommy'. Moreover, Gibson's best lyrics render personal concerns rather than grandiose ones. Such qualities allow Gibson, writing quite early in the war, to point to some of its most troubling aspects. The parent of 'The Return' knows of the early euphoria –

> He went, and he was gay to go:
> And I smiled on him as he went.

– but also of anxiety:

> wondering all the while
> What stranger would come back to me.

The 'I' of 'Raining' was warned by his father that going to the war might prove a stupid thing – and lies in the trench thinking that his father was right. Gibson often seems to stage his effects, but he is registering aspects of experience which are neither heroic nor reassuring. The friend of the 'I' in 'His Mate' has gone mad on a pile of corpses:

> And, as he stopt to snigger,
> I struggled to my knees and pulled the trigger.

Gibson's best verse has an awful simplicity:

> This bloody steel
>   Has killed a man.
> I heard him squeal
> As on I ran.
> . . . . . . . . .
> Though clean and clear
>   I've wiped the steel,
> I still can hear
>   That dying squeal.

('The Bayonet')[22]

It is perhaps significant that Gibson writes directly of the bayonet – the blade on the end of the ranker's rifle – instead of retaining the sword other poets clung to. In fact, Gibson has the confidence in directness to achieve an effective alternative to the piled horrors of reportage and the vapid diffusions of Rupert Brooke; and this directness is specifically associated with the imagined responses of the underprivileged. What Gibson provides is the suggestion that such voices are of people whose confidence has been shaken and who are sensitive to the brutalities beneath the role-playing. This is not to claim that such role-playing is false or invalid, but to suggest that Gibson provides a complement, and one which insists that those who hoe or sit by peat fires have emotions and anxieties beneath the surfaces of more public postures.

Isaac Rosenberg can hardly be seen as 'Tommy'. He was a Jew of Lithuanian-Latvian origin, whose family moved from Bristol to London's East End when he was seven. He was at the Slade from 1911 to 1914. His foreign ancestry, his time at art school, and his Jewishness all mark him as exotic, although both his working-class location and his education at Stepney Board School (which he left at 14) align him with hundreds of thousands of rankers – as does his service in the army. Rosenberg enlisted as a private in the King's Own Royal Lancaster Regiment in 1915 and was killed on the Western Front in 1918.

The poems grouped as 'Trench Poems 1916–1918' in Bottomley

and Harding's edition of the *Collected Poems*[23] have, broadly speaking, the sense of detachment which is seen in 'On Receiving News of the War', a poem written in 1914 in Cape Town, Rosenberg having been sent there in June of that year because of a lung condition. It is strikingly free of the easy euphoria of so many initial responses and entirely free of chauvinism. The coming of war is seen as a 'malign kiss' moulding lives and in terms of 'Red fangs' which tear God's face and shed his blood. This is a rewriting of ideas of cleansing, although the last stanza may be an appeal for a corrosive purification to be the outcome of the conflict:

> O! ancient crimson curse!
> Corrode, consume.
> Give back this universe
> Its pristine bloom.

This, however, is more reminiscent of John Donne's 'Holy Sonnets' than of Rupert Brooke.

The detachment and independence of Rosenberg are evident at various levels, from the bitterness of 'The Jew' –

> The blonde, the bronze, the ruddy,
> With the same heaving blood,
> Keep tide to the moon of Moses.
> Then why do they sneer at me?

– to the sense of the damage war brings:

> Iron are our lives
> Molten right through our youth.
> A burnt space through ripe fields
> A fair mouth's broken tooth.

('August 1914')

Where Binyon might see the renewal of natural rhythms and Owen concentrates upon the redness of lips, Rosenberg sees the burning and the broken tooth.

Rosenberg seems also to reach instinctively (or culturally) for that which undercuts ideals. In 'The Dying Soldier', the soldier asks for

> Water – water – O water
> For one of England's dying sons.

The situation is reminiscent of the story of the injured Sir Philip Sidney giving his water-flask to a soldier on the battlefield of Zutphen, but here there is no such solace:

'We cannot give you water
Were all England in your breath'.
'Water – water – O water'
He moaned and swooned to death.

Brooke's soldier was England transcendent and his 'dust' was seen as an enrichment to 'some foreign field'. Here there is only the elemental moaning, and death.

In 'The Dead Heroes', of 1915, Rosenberg writes (much more convincingly than usual) of soldiers as 'they'; as other than himself:

Their blood is England's heart;
By their dead hands
It is their noble part
That England stands.

But the position of the persona in 'Marching' is different. The perspective is very precisely given by the sub-title – 'As seen from the left file'. Yet there is strong emphasis on the singular:

My eyes catch ruddy necks
Sturdily pressed back –
All a red brick moving glint.

When, in the second stanza, there is a plural first person pronoun it describes observers rather than the marching troops:

We husband the ancient glory
In these bared necks and hands.

This poet-figure is one of the troops, but not in the sense of being incorporated. There is a similar limit to identification in the famous 'Break of Day in the Trenches'. The poet-figure's hand that touches the 'queer sardonic rat' is 'this English hand', but it is 'they' who would shoot the rat if 'they knew/Your cosmopolitan sympathies'. Yet, while it is tempting to see the poet-figure as identifying with the rat rather than with 'Strong eyes, fine limbs, haughty athletes', Rosenberg knows that his poet-figure cannot be finally divorced from other combatants: 'What do you see in our eyes?'. This tension between 'they' and 'ours' is characteristic and revealing. Many who wrote about the war noted the rats; only Rosenberg finds them appealing.

Even where identification is simpler, the effect is of detachment. 'Louse Hunting' begins like notes –

Nudes – stark and glistening,

> Yelling in lurid glee. Grinning faces
> And raging limbs
> Whirl over the floor one fire. . . .

– and closes in on 'Yon soldier' before moving to the 'We' which dominates the second stanza: 'we all sprang up and stript/To hunt the verminous brood'. Yet the imperative and repeated 'See' suggests an urging by a non-participant. In 'Dead Man's Dump' (which is, in the full sense of the word, one of the most awful poems of the war) the play of pronouns makes a dance of sympathy, brutality and guilt. The dead are 'they' ('Burnt black by strange decay/Their sinister faces lie') and can be presented almost in terms of a conducted tour: 'Here is one not long dead'. But such a degree of detachment, the poem's honesty knows, is not valid. There is an 'us' in the poem which wonders about its fate ('What of us who, flung on the shrieking pyre,/Walk, our usual thoughts untouched?') and which is present as the arrival at the poem's end. The last questions are 'Will they come? Will they ever come?', and the deliverance is the 'we' who 'crashed round the bend':

> We heard his weak scream,
> We heard his very last sound,
> And our wheels grazed his dead face.

The poem's sense of what it is to damage and be damaged is complex, in ways which go far beyond nationalistic antagonisms and loyalties and which bring victims, rescuers and destroyers into a terrible symbiosis.

Gibson seems clear about his identifications: Rosenberg markedly less so. It is tempting to explain the latter's insecurity by his Jewishness ('why do they sneer at me?'). Yet 'insecurity' is not quite accurate, for Rosenberg writes with considerable confidence and assurance, and the effect of his verse is not of idiosyncrasy or neurosis. Rather, beyond the compression and allusiveness, there is certainty and, instead of protest, a kind of acceptance. The sensibility that receives 'news of the war' with the remark that 'Snow is a strange white word' is scarcely receiving news at all – except of what, since it has happened before, is natural and expected, even though ghastly.

This acceptance is very different from the lightweight and irresponsible view that war is glibly part of God's masterplan, provides a 'natural' winnowing, or a precious opportunity for heroism. It is also distinct from the grumbling but finally patient and stoical Tommy of the Bairnsfather account. Yet, even though Rosenberg's roots are so obviously in the history of the Jews and their mechanisms for coping with successive disasters, it is the tough patience he survives by that provides a link between his poetry, with its individual accent, and the concept of a ranker-voice. Rosenberg utters the voice of those who endure: 'We're here because we're here because we're here because we're here'. So he is finally part of a 'we' and that, rather than his Jewishness, is his importance.

Ivor Gurney came from a very different background. He was the son of a Gloucester tailor; was educated as a chorister at King's School, Gloucester; and won an Open Scholarship to the Royal College of Music. Not many manage this – certainly few from Gurney's background – and he seems to have struck people as unusual. Patrick Kavanagh cites his sister's remark that Ivor 'did not seem to belong to us', while Marion Scott's attention was initially caught by his 'thick, dark blue Severn pilot's coat, more suggestive of an out-of-door life than the composition lesson with Sir Charles Stanford'. She also remarked on the 'look of latent force in him'. Stanford was later to comment that Gurney was potentially 'the biggest' of his pupils, but the 'least teachable'.[24] By 1914 Gurney was setting poems to music and beginning to write verse of his own. He volunteered, was rejected because of his eyesight, but accepted into the ranks in 1915, serving as a private throughout the rest of the war, during which he was slightly wounded and gassed. Gurney was thus a ranker, but of an unusual sort, clearly a talented man who had already had success and who had moved, both literally and metaphorically, some way from his background by the time the war accepted him.

Gurney shows considerable awareness of the ranker's position in the military hierarchy. The sonnet 'Servitude', quoted earlier, speaks of 'this brass-cleaning life' and of 'sergeant-major's bluster and noise'. It is important to note that the sonnet registers oppression without seeming depressed: the linking of the sergeant-major with brass, hell-fire and guns seems humorous rather than anything else, as is the firm refusal to respond to the suggestion of an officer with 'the politest voice – a finicking accent' in 'The Silent One'. Similarly, in 'The Bohemians', those who 'would not clean their buttons,/Nor polish buckles after latest fashions' are objects of a rich, if grim joke: they 'died off one by one, or became officers'. This humour suggests self-confidence, a sense of identity and a degree of detachment, which shade into shrewd experience in 'Of Grandcourt'. Here a friend of the poet-figure suggests they volunteer for the Front, rather than staying in 'Grandcourt trenches reserve' because the latter is even worse than the former – 'But I had seen too many ditches and stood too long/Feeling my feet freeze, and my shoulders ache'. The poet-figure adds that there is a difference between himself and his friend: 'he was Lance Corporal and might be full Corporal'. The voice is that of the ranker using his experience of the war to avoid danger and discomfort where possible: in the circumstances of the war 'a thought less danger' was important, if hardly heroic.

These, clearly, are not heroic voices, but although they could scarcely appeal to Henry Newbolt, they have authority and knowingness. Moreover, Gurney shows a sense of self as part of a group. 'On a Two-Hundredth Birthday' has a parenthesis which glances back on the war ('we in hacked-up Flanders'):

> (Raikes, that kind-thoughted, gay man, had laughed,
> We sitting there in drips of rain to ponder
> On small home businesses, so mired and chill.)

In 'Near Vermand' this sense of identity extends to the claim to know the collective desire:

> And we were in forced marches after an enemy pressed
> Through snowstorms and such, seeking an end to this ending.
> But an order took us on, we were led. . . .

Yet Gurney avoids claiming to speak for an abstraction like Tommy, and the sense of difference that applies to his perceptions of rank is also present in his consideration of being a ranker among rankers. This is movingly and precisely pinned down in 'Farewell':

> There was not one of all that battalion
> Loved his comrades as well as I – but kept shy.
> Or said in verse, what his voice would not rehearse.

This sense of self is what allows Gurney to comment on his fellow-rankers at times as if he were an outsider. In 'Song' ('I had a girl's fancies') we have

> So, to the admiration
> Of the rough high virtues
> Of common marching

> Soldiers, and textures
> Of russet noblenesses,
> My mind was turned. . . .

'While I Write' speaks similarly of how 'the common goodness of those soldiers shown day after day . . . Stays with me yet'. This is not idealisation: notice the precise tension in 'rough high virtues' and 'common goodness'. But if the poet-voices claim individuality, they insist on granting the same to other rankers, as with the quick characterisation of Raikes in 'On a Two-Hundredth Birthday' and in the recognition of difference in 'Of Grandcourt'. The dialogic relationship between the individual and the group is nicely caught in 'Billet', where 'one Private took on himself a Company's heart to speak'. The phrase 'took on himself' keeps the idea that this is a presumption, the catching and voicing of a moment of identity which does not cancel difference.

Gurney's sense of separateness or individuality in the ranks is one of the most important features of his war poems, for the recognition that 'the men' are not a mere mass is a necessary critique of the mentality from which wars come. It is made the more precise, however, by Gurney's awareness of the pressures towards uniformity: 'an order took us on, we were led' ('Near Vermand'). This sensitivity appears again with the warmth with which welcomes are recorded:

> Then we were taken in
> To low huts candle-lit, shaded close by slitten
> Oilsheets, and there the boys gave us kind welcome. . . .
>
>                              ('First Time In' (1))

The vitality which Gurney's poems communicate goes far beyond the sentimental; and this is partly so because the alert observation that comments with such awful affection on the 'Infinite lovely chatter of Bucks accent' of a man who 'died on the wires, and hung there, one of two' ('The Silent One') is the same as that which responds to welcome here:

> And then one took us courteously
> Where a sheet lifted, and gold light cautiously
> Streamed from an oilsheet slitted vertical. . . .
>
>                              ('First Time In' (2))

And this alertness is also what makes Gurney the great communicator of basic facts of ranker experience – the marching, the fatigue, the weight of equipment; the luxury of rest and a good billet. Much of this is epitomised in the brief 'After War':

> One got peace of heart at last, the dark march over,
> And the straps slipped, the warmth felt under roof's low cover,
> Lying slack the body, let sink in straw giving;
> And some sweetness, a great sweetness left in mere living. . . .

The ability to sense the 'sweetness . . . in mere living' is one of Gurney's great gifts, and is what makes his best verse vital even where heart-breaking. But two other points about these lines are important. Simple details like 'the straps slipped' do much to establish authenticity, and this is reinforced by what might, more formalistically, be seen as a defect – the elliptical notation so common in Gurney's writing: 'Lying slack the body, let sink in straw giving' – such shorthand is very precise indeed.

It may be a necessary paradox to say that Gurney speaks for the ranker more convincingly than any other poet of the war because he does not think of his poet-voices as versions of the Ranker. It is, perhaps, precisely because Gurney has a sense of, and respect for, individuality that he is able to identify moments and areas of common cause so convincingly. Beyond this, it is difficult to say exactly why the voices of so many of Gurney's war poems seem so authentic. He does not write dialect, as John Clare had done, but he shares Clare's love of the feeling of words, and he exploits the limitations of the signifier : signified relationship, making words work hard to articulate impressions: 'The dark barn roof, and the glows and the wedges and streaks' ('After War'). What is most striking, perhaps, is how assured Gurney seems linguistically, at least once he has burnt off his early poetic self-consciousness. The war was a disaster for Ivor Gurney, but he entered it at a point where he was perhaps perfectly poised between tailor's son and composer at the Royal College of Music. Rather as he seems unintimidated by superior rank and able to hold his individuality in the ranks, he appears able to celebrate his roots and to exploit the culture his talent opened up to him.

## NOTES

1. *The Age of Empire*, p. 156.
2. *England 1865-1914*, Longman, 1979, p. 89.

3. J. Lawson and H. Silver, *A Social History of Education in England*, Methuen, 1973, p. 324ff.
4. P. Thompson, *The Edwardians* (1975), Paladin, 1977, p. 199.
5. *Letters from the Front*, Dent, 1975, p. 3.
6. *With a machine gun from Cambrai*, HMSO, 1969.
7. *War Poems and Others*, ed. D. Hibberd (1973), Chatto and Windus, 1977, p. 107.
8. *More songs by the fighting men*, p. 64.
9. Hibbert/Onions, p. 76.
10. *More songs . . .*, p. 38.
11. ibid. p. 39.
12. Osborn, *The Muse . . .*, p. 285.
13. ibid. p. 291.
14. ibid. p. 288.
15. pp. 7, 9–10, 13.
16. All in *Ballads of Battle*.
17. Both in *Work-a-Day Warriors*.
18. All in *Work-a-Day Warriors*.
19. ibid.
20. Osborn, *The Muse . . .*, pp. ix–xi.
21. Hibberd/Onions, p. 217.
22. All Gibson quotations are from *Battle*.
23. Chatto and Windus (1937), 1977, from which all the Rosenberg quotations are taken.
24. *Collected Poems*, ed. P. J. Kavanagh, Introduction, p. 5. All the Gurney quotations in this section are from this edition.

## 5

# BELIEF AND WILFRED OWEN

## WAR AND CHIVALRY

In 1916 *The Times* printed Eleanor Alexander's poem 'Who Sleeps', which seeks to unite men and women, combatants and non-combatants, into a single nation which 'will keep/The flag of England clean' and which is endorsed by a god ('Captain of hosts and our Salvation') who 'slumbers not nor sleeps'.[1] In the second stanza the poet imagines the bride who 'girt' her husband and was 'Gay when her happy warrior went', while the ninth considers those

> who forge for England's care
> Armour laid on the anvil of her soul
> And hammered out with prayer.

Alberta Vickridge has a poem ('In a V.A.D. Pantry') which offers a cup as a 'humble Grail' to 'Lips of fever, parched for drink'. Margaret Colvin sees love as transforming 'the bitter cup' of war into 'the Holy Grail' ('Our Blessed Slain', 1914). Beatrix Brice speaks of the BEF standing fast while England 'girt her armour on' ('To the Vanguard', 1914) and Katharine Tynan presents 'Your son and my son' dreaming 'of knight's armour', of 'Bugles and trumpets' ('To the Others').[2]

If these details are examined in terms of realism they are clearly, so far as the First World War is concerned, anachronistic and more or less absurd. The sword was a badge of the officer, but of limited practical use in the war, while it had been over 250 years since even a reduced version of knightly armour had been relevant to warfare. But this is scarcely pertinent to such usages as those quoted above, which have more to do with codes of behaviour and attitudes of mind than with the practical details of early twentieth-century fighting. Girding on armour becomes a symbolic act of arming to defend the country and the right: in Tynan's poem this is figured as a crusade. Colvin seeks to transform the 'bitter cup' of war-as-crucifixion into the Grail quest, in which the successful quester has, like Galahad, a divine revelation. Since there was such a enormous gap between the shining armour and prancing steeds of the worlds of chivalric romance and the khaki-and-mud reality of the trenches, it is perhaps as well that the examples quoted above are so generalised.

The effort to see this early modern war as a chivalric enterprise is, of course, an effort at preparation and then consolation; making the conflict bearable by reading it as purposive and divinely sanctioned (so far as *our* participation is concerned), whereby the sacrifices are made worthwhile and salvation is the reward. There is also a further dimension where the poet is, as in the given examples, a woman. Alexander is concerned with the female role in the chivalric situations she invokes, calling on Florence Nightingale and the biblical Rachel, as well as the personified figures of Bride, Mother and even Barren Woman. Her bride serves by arming and sending out her husband to battle and her Nightingale provides solace for the wounded, serving like Vickridge's VAD. The roles imagined are at root close enough to women's actual experience of the war. Even Alexander's armourers could be women in the munitions factories, though preparing shells rather than plate armour or chain mail. In chivalric romance, moreover, knights were inspired by, and fought for, ladies, who thus had responsibility to and for them.

But male poets also felt the need to see the war in such terms. Bertram Dobell addresses the Belgian General Leman as

> A man of men; cast in the selfsame mould
> As Bayard and our Sidney. . . .
>
> ('To General Leman')

The Germans have offered a challenge: 'The gauntlet we must needs take up' ('Marching Song').[3] Henry Chappell has volunteers hearing 'the tocsin's call' and grasping 'the brand'.[4] Dobell died just after the war began, while Chappell seems to have been a non-combatant. Rather more interesting are the combatants who use this language.

One of these is Herbert Asquith (son of the Prime Minister Henry Asquith, and educated at Winchester and Balliol). His volunteer is a clerk 'Toiling at ledgers in a city grey', 'With no lance broken in life's tournament', who, however, breaks his lance in the war, having become, in effect, a knight by the act of volunteering.

W.N. Hodgson, who was killed on the first day on the Somme, hears 'Sons of mine' thrilling 'To the trumpet call of war' and exhorts them to 'Gird'. Corporal Howard Spring presents his unsung dead lying with 'Buckler broken, sword unslung'. In the spring of 1918 F.W.D. Bendall, who reached the rank of colonel, wrote 'A Outrance', a poem which is shot through with the language of chivalry – gage, lists, trumpets:

> Her knights are in the field,
>   His blade each warrior draws,
> Their pride – a stainless shield –
>   Their strength – a righteous cause.[5]

Bendall's account is reminiscent of John Arkwright's volume, *The Supreme Sacrifice*. I do not know whether or not Arkwright was a combatant, but his volume offers an account of the combatant as knight. It has illustrations by Bairnsfather and Louis Raemaekers, as well as by Lunt and Raven-Hill, and these graphically underline Arkwright's version of the war. So the brief poem 'The Young Knight' is faced by Raven-Hill's drawing of a fully-armed young man, holding up his reversed sword, dedicating it to 'this the holiest; last Crusade!'. Another drawing by Raven-Hill, for the poem 'France's Day', represents France in plate armour and shield, while Raemaekers illustrates 'The Crumbling Shield' as being held by a flinching Attila, battered by a knight with a cross on *his* shield.

Chivalry need not be seen simply in the context of war, but it is rooted in ideas of conflict between males. It includes ideas of proper behaviour to females, but, although in the chivalric code women should inspire and encourage men to chivalric action, these actions are exclusive to males. Thus, in Malory, Lancelot acts to protect Guinevere, who is herself passive. The actions of the chivalric knight are usually violent – in tournament, man-to-man combat, battle – but the code demands fair fighting, respect for your opponent and the display of mercy. Chivalry is ideal behaviour; it is strongly anachronistic and mythical in tendency; and it stands at a variable distance from actuality. One of its focusings is on the idea of King Arthur and his Round Table. The very lack of solid knowledge of this shadowy nationalist facilitates the elaboration of legend, but the most famous early English representations of Arthurian chivalry fail to conceal that the ideals are laid over brutal actualities. Malory seems to be seeking to revive chivalry and is drawn to idealisation, but lust and bloodshed mark his pages. In *Sir Gawain and the Green*

*Knight* the anonymous poet has Gawain as the proper bearer of the pentangle, and thus of its ideals, but knightly fear runs through the poem. Rape and cruel indifference to inflicting pain are prominent in Spenser's *The Faerie Queene*.

The strength of such accounts lies in the tensions between the visions and the grasp of actualities, but Spenser, writing in the last quarter of the sixteenth century, can only present chivalry in a 'faerie' landscape. Tudor tournaments were increasingly distant from military realities: Sidney died of a bullet wound. The nineteenth-century revival of chivalry had to be an exercise in costume drama, although, it is not the less significant for that. Tennyson's 'The Charge of the Light Brigade' marks the futility of cavalry charges in the face of modern cannon (not that the poem recognises this). Girouard has detailed chivalry's revival in the decades before the war in his *The Return to Camelot*, but the trappings cannot properly cover the realities of an increasingly urban – industrial society, unless they are generalised to the point reached by Eleanor Alexander:

> They sleep not for whom furnace smoke-clouds roll
> Nor they who forge for England's care,
> Armour. . . .

('Who Sleeps')

The desire to believe that 'we' were involved in a chivalric war is understandable enough. It is the positive to those negatives of propaganda that present the Germans as Attila or Antichrist. But the imagery of chivalry was inevitably very vulnerable in the Great War. Horses, lances and swords were the last physical links with the Age of Chivalry, but horses (and therefore lances) had a bad war, and by its end the tank was marking the passing of cavalry. As for the sword, it rapidly gave way to the brutal effectiveness of the bayonet. Moreover, to read about bayonet-drill is to become aware of how necessarily unchivalrous this war was. One major reality was shelling at long range, while close-quarter encounters suggest the filth of Agincourt, rather than anything like elegant and colourful joustings. What this means is simply that, at the level of physical experience, chivalry had little to offer and could hardly be used as analysis (except perhaps satirically). So the Raven-Hill and Raemaekers drawings mentioned above exclude recognisable war detail completely. Where such detail is found in Arkwright's volume (as notably with Bairnsfather's illustrations for 'The Pilgrim's Way') picture and poem are referentially separate. It can also be suggested that the gap was so great that the attempt to read the one in terms of the other could scarcely remain convincing even at the level of metaphor. Knights do not sit in muddy dugouts being shelled at long distance or struggle across No Man's Land towards machine guns and wire; and since they don't, knights readily cease to be relevant. Bairnsfather was the most popular British artist of the war and one of the illustrators of Arkwright's volume. But his greatest creation was no Galahad. He was instead the scruffy Old Bill. Bairnsfather's cartoon 'That Sword', a diptych, sums up the death of chivalry: in the second part the symbol of chivalry is being used to toast bread.[6]

It is difficult to see how concepts of chivalry could have survived for long in the trenches or at sea in ironclads, with the subversive torpedo and, again, long-distance shelling; although aerial combat could more readily be seen in these terms. But even civilians, with censorship restricting their access to war news, encountered in photographs and cartoons, poems and – most nakedly – in casualty lists, evidence that chivalry did not provide a tenable account of the war. There are, in fact, relatively few sustained accounts of the war as chivalric, although many poems use some language ultimately derived from chivalry, and such efforts – even where as elaborate as in Arkwright's volume – are only ideologically convincing in the absence of thought. Tynan's sons might dream of knightly armour, but the impressive dreams from the war are nightmares.

Humbert Wolfe has a 1918 poem, 'To Him whom the Cap fits'.[7] It has an Arthurian epitaph: ' "What sword is left" sighs England. Answer her (for you must answer) "This – Excalibur" '. Excalibur, Wolfe's poem says at its start, is 'the sword of England', but his first sonnet offers a catalogue of failures – at the defeat of Harold at Hastings, the execution of Charles I, and the death of William Pitt, for example. Here Excalibur, the sword of Arthur himself, is associated with defiance in the face of disaster:

> . . . only those who in defeat have known
> The bitterness of death, and stood alone
> In darkness, shall have worship in the grave.
> Swordsman, go into battle, and record
> How one more English knight has found his sword!

This is the voice of the end of 'The Battle of Maldon', a way of making the Arthurian motif compatible with Ypres and Passchendaele.

Isolating the chivalric motif, as I have done so far, does, however, distort its value for some poets of the war, in so far as the theme is commonly one which works in combination with others, rather than in isolation. Of itself, chivalry comes to be so distant from experience as to be rapidly vacuous, even offensive. Its comforts could not last, but when chivalric ideals form part of a combination they prove more durable. They frequently combine with the contemplation of Christ and his crucifixion, for example, and this combination can come closer to the realities than chivalry alone could ever be. The link has already been intimated: the Grail quest associates the Arthurian stories with the blood of Christ; Raemaekers's knight has Christ's cross upon his shield; Tynan's chivalric sons hear trumpets calling to 'the Holy War' – they are 'clean as new swords' and are destined 'for the Great Crusade,/With the banner of Christ over them – our knights new-made'.[8] These quotations from Tynan make the point about combination, associating rebirth, cleanliness, chivalric armour, the crusades and Christ in a subliminally rich mixture.

## CHRIST AND THE CROSS

The cross, that brutal prop of Roman punishment of criminals, became a central symbol for Christianity with its use for the execution of Jesus Christ. Its symbolism depends upon the narrative of the Messiah going beyond defeat on the cross to victory in resurrection and ascension. Since Christ, as Son of God, is crucified to redeem the Fall, and since Christ is a volunteer for redemptive crucifixion, the cross is, for the Christian, a symbol of hope and a guarantee that there is purpose and pattern in human life.

Paul Fussell has reminded us of 'the numerous real physical calvaries visible at French and Belgian crossroads'.[9] Such images of Christ crucified may have made a particular impression on British soldiers because they are not common phenomena in Britain. Most of these soldiers were, notionally, Protestants, moving through alien Catholic landscapes. Certainly, the poets notice the crosses. Geoffrey Dearmer's, however, are not shrines but the crosses on graves at Gallipoli:

Before me ugly shapes like spectres stand,

And wooden crosses cleave the waning light
('From 'W' Beach')

as are those of J. Griffyth Fairfax:

Cross after cross, mound after mound. . . .
('The Forest of the Dead')[10]

Patrick MacGill, however, presents a church crucifix in the wreck of the village of Givenchy:

mute upon the crucifix He looks upon it all –
The great white Christ, the shrapnel-scourged, upon the eastern
wall.
('A Soldier's Prayer')[11]

Crucifixion has a special horror in Christianity because of the blasphemy of the execution of the Son of God. To be identified with the killers of Christ is to be a blasphemer and the enemy of God; and so it is hardly surprising that crucifixion plays its part in the propaganda of the Great War. J.M. Read tells us that 'the report that soldiers and babies were crucified by the "Huns" . . . came out in the British papers not long after the first use of gas on the western front (April 22, 1915)'.[12] The dating is interesting. Use of gas by the Germans was seen as 'beastliness', final confirmation that the enemy was not 'playing the game'; was, in fact, a Christ-killer. When, according to Read, the question of German crucifixions was discussed in the House of Commons for the second time, the MP who raised the issue provided details: 'the Germans had removed the figure of Christ from the large village crucifix and fastened the sergeant while alive to the cross'. As late as September 1917 a story of German crucifixions of Canadian soldiers was used to support the case for American entry into the war. At this point it is enough to note that to identify Germans with Christ-killers is to facilitate transfer to that race of anti-Semitic sentiments (which were sadly strong in Britain and elsewhere). It follows that war with Germany is war against the enemies of the Christian God, a crusade; while the alleged crucifixion of soldiers encourages the idea of the soldier as a surrogate Christ.

In terms of patterning, Christ and his crucifixion offer two main, potentially sustaining readings of the war. If the soldier is actually identified with Christ, he has 'put on the armour of God' and is fighting to save mankind. His death will be followed by resurrection and victory. If Christ is seen as present at the scene of the conflict (even if not identical with the soldier) this will be the guarantee that 'our' cause is righteous and will triumph. In either case the war is holy, has pattern and purpose – to defeat the powers of darkness. But it should be added that the full significance of the icon of Christ-crucified depends on interpreting it in the context of the total pattern of Christ's life – the rejections and humiliations as well as the triumphs. What conclusions you draw may depend upon how much of the story you choose to tell, and where you stop.

Some versions of the crucifixion in poetry of the war are quite simple. MacGill's 'A Soldier's Prayer', for example, sees the war as replaying Christ's execution. It is the mark of humankind's ingratitude to Christ: 'And as men scourged Him long ago, they scourge Him once again' – but Christ continues to pity 'his children's wrath, their passion and their crime', and so the soldier's prayer is to Christ to 'Forgive the ones who work Thee harm. O Lord, forgive us all'. Yet MacGill's simplicity is at least not the simplistic propaganda version: the damage war does (the recrucifixion of Christ) is not, as in the comfortable version, the fault of the Germans alone. Humankind is Christ's enemy and needs forgiveness.

Catherine Reilly says that Lucy Whitmell's 'Christ in Flanders' (originally published in September 1915, in *The Spectator*) was 'reprinted widely and became one of the most popular and most anthologised poems of the war'.[13] 1915 was the year of second Ypres and Gallipoli (both in April) and of Loos (which began days after the poem's first appearance). It was also the year of the Bryce report on German atrocities. But Whitmell's poem avoids abusing the Germans directly or directly identifying them as killers of Christ. It presents Christ in the context of the crucifixion, and Christ is clearly on 'our' side:

> . . . we know that You are here.
> . . . . . . . . . . .
> You helped us pass the jest along the trenches –
> Where, in cold blood, we waited in the trenches –
>     You touched its ribaldry and made it fine.
> You stood beside us in our pain and weakness. . . .

The fourth stanza associates 'us' with England, but the poem, while suggesting that Christ's crucifixion was for this 'us' ('We know You prayed for us upon the Cross'), ends with the ideas that 'we' need pardoning and that Christ will stay faithful in a trial of endurance which is some way from patriotism or Holy War.

Iris Tree comes closer than Whitmell to identifying the soldier with Christ:

> Of all who died in darkness far away
> Nothing is left of them but LOVE, who triumphs now,
> His arms held crosswise to the budding day,
> The passion-red roses clustering his brow.

('Poem untitled')

Like Whitmell, however, and like Muriel Stuart, her version largely ignores the enemy. Stuart's is the 'unknown soldier':

>                 this forgotten dead
> Went out into the night alone.

– 'He gave, as Christ, the life he had' and gives rise, in his death, to communion:

> There was his body broken for you,
> There was his blood divinely shed
> That in the earth lie lost and dim.
> Eat, drink. . . .

('Forgotten Dead I Salute You')[14]

Such poems, which logically imply that the enemy is the killer of Christ, yet refrain from making the point directly, their reticence (and Whitmell's call for pardon) perhaps suggesting that the guilt for this war went beyond the platitudes of patriotism. Eden Phillpotts, however, recalls the propagandists in his sonnet 'To Belgium':[15]

> Though coward hands have nailed you to the tree
> And shed your innocent blood and dug your grave,
> Rejoice and live!

(In fairness, Phillpotts, who was over 50 in 1914, had had little opportunity to go beyond the propaganda. What remains depressing, however, is the failure to see any complexity in the situation which had led to the war.) The padre Studdert Kennedy asks in 'Her Gift' what Calvary means in the context of seeing 'men die/Not once, nor twice, but many times/In agony/As ghastly to behold as that'.[16] In Kennedy's poem one of those who died is Rob McNeil, who, dying, 'pleaded with his men/To take that gun,/And kill the Hun/That worked it, dead'. In context, McNeil could scarcely be expected to offer any other advice, but the suggestion of vengeance, if linked with the opening enquiry about the meaning of Calvary, produces a nasty version of crucifixion and Christianity.

But, remembering how often crosses enter the poetry of the war, it is striking how seldom they make a pattern of execration of the enemy. The level and complexity of response may vary greatly but the tendency is to turn inwards to endurance or self-doubt, rather than to bring Christ in on 'our' side in confidence that 'we' are his chosen and the enemy the select of Satan.

Richard Aldington's 'Battlefield' exemplifies one form which turning inwards can take.[17] The poem's landscape is familar enough:

> this shell-rent ground;
> Every house in sight
> Is smashed and desolate

but something grows in this barrenness:

> in this fruitless land,
> Thorny with wire
> And foul with rotting clothes and sacks,
> The crosses flourish –
> Ci-git, ci-git, ci-git . . .
> "Ci-git 1 soldat Allemand,
> *Priez pour lui.*"

Aldington's poem is poised for ironical readings. The memorials to dead soldiers are all that grow here, but the reference to praying at least intimates hope. In this case an English poet represents a French voice praying for a German corpse. The atomisations of nationalism have given way to the community of 'shell-rent ground' and the grave.

The symbolist nature of Aldington's poem allows transcendence of its own negatives: there may be salvation in trans-national empathy. But it was suggested above that a reading of the crucifixion with reference to the war depends on where you stop, what aspects of the whole pattern you focus on. Siegfried Sassoon has a short and early (March 1916) poem which ends:

> The sentry keeps his watch where no one stirs
> But the brown rats, the nimble scavengers.

Sassoon provides a gloss: 'Written in trenches. The weather beastly wet and the place was like the end of the world.' The poem is called 'Golgotha', where, for Christians, the world would have ended had Christ's crucifixion not been followed by the resurrection.[18] Sassoon does nothing, however, to encourage a reader to see the association of

Golgotha and trench as anything beyond two places of skulls. The freezing of the sequence which this represents occurs more forcefully in Rudyard Kipling's 'Gethsemane (1914-1918)'.[19] The title connects the garden where Christ was arrested with the contemporary world of war, and the poem then elaborates:

> The Garden called Gethsemane
>   In Picardy it was,
> And there the people came to see
>   The English soldiers pass.

The poet-figure echoes Christ ('I prayed my cup might pass') but, like Christ, finds no escape:

> It didn't pass for me,
> I drank it when we met the gas
>   Beyond Gethsemane.

Here the sequence made up of Christ's journey to and into crucifixion is superimposed on the soldier's experience. But there is no resurrection and the buoyancy of Kipling's rhythms presents only a dance of death.

Kipling's reference to gas could be read as identifying Germans with Christ-killers, but Christ's plea that the cup might pass has less to do with his executioners as individuals than with the burden of suffering brought upon him by human sinfulness at large. The gospel accounts of the crucifixion are not racist, nor does Kipling's poem seem so. It is the condition of experiencing the war which is concentrated on, and a famous letter by Wilfred Owen shows where this could lead:

> For 14 hours yesterday I was at work – teaching Christ to lift his cross by numbers, and how to adjust his crown; and not to imagine he thirst till after the last halt. I attended his Supper to see that there were no complaints; and inspected his feet that they should be worthy of the nails. I see to it that he is dumb, and stands at attention before his accusers. With a piece of silver I buy him every day, and with maps I make him familiar with the topography of Golgotha.[20]

Here, first of all, the 'I' is not Christ, but the officer as instrument, almost theatrical producer – 'teaching Christ to lift his cross by numbers, and how to adjust his crown'. This shades into the officer as someone like a priest preparing the sacrificial victim ('inspected his feet to see that they should be worthy of the nails') and then into the officer as Judas, 'with a piece of silver I buy him every day'. The ranker is Christ, prepared for and betrayed into crucifixion by his officer. In this passage Owen comes close to identifying the true Christ-killers with himself and those whose authority, he, as officer, represents. It is only a short step to Sassoon's bayonets harrowing the hell of Home.

Herbert Read's 'My Company' is a meditation on the relationship between officers and men.[21] In the poem's second section, the officer turns to look at the rankers at their tasks:

> My men go wearily
> With their monstrous burdens.
> . . . . . . . . .
> They bear wooden planks
> And iron sheeting
> Through the area of death.

As they work they swear 'Oh bloody Christ', and the poet-figure then identifies them with the subject of their blasphemy:

> My men, my modern Christs,
> Your bloody agony confronts the world.

Cursing Christ, the soldiers thus curse themselves. The appeal implicit in the curse fails, and, as Christ's role required that he go beyond the cry 'My God, my God', so the soldiers have to labour beyond cursing. Here, again, the world is not redeemed, but merely confronted. For resurrection we are offered this:

> A man of mine
>    lies on the wire;
> And he will rot
> And first his lips
> The worms will eat.

> (Section three)

In the final section the officer also becomes (rather like a Judas) a version of Christ. He 'can assume/A giant attitude and godlike mood', but 'Then again I assume/My human docility,/Bow my head/And share their doom'. In so far as the officer can only finally participate in the rankers' doom he cannot solve the enigma of this dual role; and cannot, therefore, hope to solve the enigma of Christ's duality as that is repeated in the experience of war.

Such accounts find little consolation in the idea that Christ is present, in or alongside, the combatant. They make little of concepts of a nationalist Christ and little of crusade ideas. Owen is troubled that he may be Judas, and Read finds comfort only in identification with 'his' men. Others find it possible to be more positive in their versions of Christ in the war. In prose, the combatant James Taylor can write: 'I seem buoyed up by . . . the constant presence of Christ',[22] and the patriotic non-combatant E.B. Osborn writes confidently of one of his 'young heroes of this warlike awakening' who 'won that cross of wood which is nobler far than any earthly order, for it is the eternal symbol of willing self-sacrifice'.[23] In verse Gurney's friend F.W. Harvey is aware that 'what men do' recrucifies Christ and appeals to him to 'let fall on this accursed place' a 'single thread of heaven that we may trace/Some way to Right!'. Yet, in so far as this suggests less confidence than Osborn shows, it is contradicted by a closing line which affirms resolution: 'Here are a thousand Christs ready to die!'.[24]

These versions identify Christ and soldier with various results. The tendency in most of the examples given to refrain from naming the enemy as anti-Christ may have something to do with the knowledge that both sides, at least formally Christian, claimed God's support. Certainly, a poem like Whitmell's would need very little change to be a *German* account. But, at times, the idea of God's support reaches the point of alleging the actual presence of Christ, or some other representative of God, on 'your' side in battle. Arthur Machen's story 'The Bowmen' is a famous example, while another is James Clark's picture 'The Great Sacrifice', which shows a dead officer on the ground, with the crucified Christ looking down on him. The title would apply to both Christ and officer, but the important point is that the Christ figure is not in the sky. The soldier's right hand is touching Christ's feet and the cross is firmly set in the same ground that the soldier is lying on. The battlefield is a Golgotha.

In Harvey's poem 'The Stranger' Christ is seen as visiting a battlefield, but the setting is 'a blood-red hell ringed round with golden weather', the context's hellishness suggesting the harrowing of hell.[25] The title's stranger is not fully identified at first, but in the fourth stanza we read

> Red, red were his hands and feet and a great hole in his side,
> Yet glory seemed to blaze about his head

and this is clearly the crucified Christ. Two stanzas earlier, the stranger had asked the poet-figure 'What would you do with life

again . . . if one could give it?', and the answer had been 'I'd live it/
Kinder to man, truer to God each day'. Now Christ repeats the
words:

> 'Kinder to man, truer to God', he whispered, and then died;
> Falling down, arms outspread.

Christ is again crucified on this battlefield: 'died/In bloodshed, and
the darkness of clouds that groaned aghast;/With pierced hands and
a great wound in His side'. For his part, the reply of the poet-figure
suggests that the war had raised him morally, but the visitation of
Christ/stranger confirms his moral resolution and the poem ends
with the crucified Christ seen as

> a shadow ever rising up to thieve
> Sin's pleasures, and the lure of every pattern lust can weave,
> And charm of all things that can do Him wrong.

Harvey's poem has nothing to say about the enemy. Logically, his
blood-red hell must contain combatants of both sides, and nothing
suggests that Christ's visit is only to the English. War is both hell
and redemption: the poem seems content with such simplicities.

Given the context, we might initially wonder if irony is intended
in Christ's dying whisper, 'Kinder to man, truer to God', but the
poem as a whole seems to intend no irony. Sassoon's 'The Redeemer'
is, however, a trickier case, in which the tone is complex from the
start.[26] In place of Harvey's generalised 'dead men, and timbers
black with flame' and 'Flame and noise of doom', we have typical
Sassoon reportage: 'We lugged our clay-sucked boots as best we
might/Along the trench', and

> We were soaked, chilled and wretched, every one;
> Darkness; the distant wink of a huge gun.

We also, however, have such writing juxtaposed with the romantic
and fairy-tale echoes of

> the mire was deep;
> It was past twelve on a mid-winter night,
> When peaceful folk in beds lay snug asleep.

The Christ-figure appears in this particularised setting. More
accurately, the figure is revealed ('A rocket . . . lit the face of what
had been a form/Floundering in mirk') and the revelation is of a
crucified Christ:

> I say that He was Christ; stiff in the glare;
> And leaning forward from His burdening task,
> Both arms supporting it. . . .

At this stage, the figure is either Christ as a stranger, mysteriously visiting the front line, or an actual soldier transformed into Christ by his labours in the line. Clark's painting reads the cross into the battlefield, but the figure is a visitor, in the expected loincloth and crown of thorns. Sassoon's figure is a participant, labouring as the poem's soldiers labour, and the third stanza supports the idea that the rocket has revealed an actual soldier rather than a stranger:

> No thorny crown, only a woollen cap
> He wore – an English soldier, white and strong. . . .

Endurance entitles this soldier to be seen as Christ ('But to the end, unjudging, he'll endure/Horror and pain') and the poem registers the redemptive power of the crucifixion:

> I say that He was Christ, who wrought to bless
> All groping things with freedom bright as air,
> And with His mercy washed and made them fair.

The repeated 'I saw that He was Christ', however, suggests the possibility of a mistaken assertion, and the poem's vision is made uncertain as the idea of redemption is undercut in the final lines. The flame of the rocket – lexically associated with 'bright as air', 'washed' and 'fair' – 'sank, and all grew black as pitch', while the poem ends with continued laborious struggle 'in the muck', and with an anonymous blasphemy – 'O Christ Almighty, now I'm stuck!'. The voice is that of a toiling soldier, but the Christ-figure was also labouring, which short-circuits the blasphemous appeal. If redemption is not cancelled, it is at least postponed indefinitely – 'now I'm stuck!'. Wry ambiguity blurs the picture.

It would be an epigrammatic half-truth to say that, before joining up in October 1915 Wilfred Owen believed in Mother, God and Poetry. There is no evidence that his belief in his mother ever weakened, but belief in God and Poetry underwent revision. I am not concerned here with Owen's belief in the latter, it being perhaps enough to note that, while Owen retained confidence in poetry, and in himself as (at least potentially) a poet, he moved from dependence primarily on Keats and Shelley to being influenced by Siegfried Sassoon (whom he met at Craiglockhart in August 1917), before moving beyond Sassoon into areas where the latter did not go. It should be added, however, that Owen's progress as a poet is not a matter of clear stages; although it can be claimed that his poems of the war represent a dialogue between the poetic traditions he was aware of and the experiences he was undergoing. Another way of making this point would be to see the relevant poems as an enquiry into how, and how far, tradition could be sustained or renovated in the face of experience. In 'A Terre' the contemplation of trench experience leads to the thought that 'Microbes have their joys,/And subdivide, and never come to death', at which point Shelley enters the poem:

> 'I shall be one with nature, herb, and stone,'
> Shelley would tell me.[27]

The second line quoted is completed by the words 'Shelley would be stunned', although this astonishment does not arise because Shelley would be shocked by the conditions being described, but because his thought has become commonplace: 'The dullest Tommy hugs that fancy now'. Here, Shelley acts as a source of philosophical nourishment, whose Romantic observation has been validated by war experience.

On 4 January 1913 Wilfred Owen wrote to Susan Owen from Dunsden Vicarage, where he was working as unpaid lay assistant to the vicar, that 'Murder will out, and I have murdered my false creed. If a true one exists, I shall find it. If not, adieu to the still falser creeds that hold the hearts of nearly all my fellow men'. It is a self-conscious, almost melodramatic statement, but this does not discredit it, and its manner is consistent with the sonnet 'Maundy Thursday'. Hibberd says that this 'may . . . be taken as a fairly light-hearted comment on Roman Catholic practices rather than as serious criticism of religion in general'. Perhaps so, but it reads to me as distanced rather than jocular, and as containing a mildly blasphemous element of adolescent daring. What emerges is awareness that the poem's silver cross has meaning which varies from worshipper to worshipper. So far as the I-figure is concerned, as it kneels to the crucifix, 'The Christ was thin, and cold, and very dead' (which seems to go beyond Hibberd's 'comment on Roman Catholic practices') – 'And yet I bowed, yea, kissed – my lips did cling'. But the erotic overtones, not uncommon in Catholic mysticism, are transferred in the last line to the flesh of the priest:

> I kissed the warm live hand that held the thing.

The daringness of the transfer is, of course, underlined by the homoeroticism and the near-contempt of 'thing'.

Both letter and poem suggest that Owen's faith was at least unsettled when he went to war, and that a simple view of how Christ might be seen in the war was, from the start, unlikely. 'Le Christianisme' (?April 1917) suggests that the icons of the church are indifferent, but not impervious to the war:

> In cellars, packed-up saints lie serried,
>   Well out of hearing of our trouble.

'One Virgin still immaculate' is

> halo'd with an old tin hat,
> But a piece of hell will batter her.

The tone has something of Sassoon's cynicism, while the last line is a sceptical commentary on the superstitions about the inviolability of icons. 'At a Calvary near the Ancre' (which, though undatable, is presumably rooted in Owen's participation in fighting near Ancre in 1917) suggests, however, a role for Christ in the war. Its position is based, as Hibberd indicates, on the sayings of Christ – 'Love one another' and 'Love your enemies'. The enactors of these precepts in the poem are the soldiers:

> they who love the greater love
> Lay down their life; they do not hate.

Such soldiers are distinguished from the representatives of the church, those priests who stroll 'Near Golgotha', proud 'That they were flesh-marked by the Beast'. They are also apart from the patriots, those 'scribes' who

> on all the people shove
> And brawl allegiance to the state.

As Hibberd notes, the flesh-marking of the priests suggests that the inculcation of hatred of the Germans is the work of the devil. The true followers of Christ are the soldiers (although it is interesting, in passing, that the verb in the line 'And now the Soldiers bear with Him' is ambiguous). Yet Owen has not worked out his perception very fully. The soldiers who watched at Christ's cross were Roman soldiers, executioners of Christ. If true Christians love their enemies, how can they bear to go on killing them? Owen blurs this issue by making his soldiers passive: they 'Lay down their life'. In reality they took life as well as giving it. If one tries to think through the line that runs from Christ-crucified to Roman soldiers to English soldiers near Ancre, one is pushed near to the conclusion that these latter are re-enacting Christ's crucifixion, as much in the killing of the enemy (Christ) as in sacrificing themselves (as Christs).

These, clearly enough, are poems of disillusion about established religion, and, in the case of 'At a Calvary. . . ', some confusion. In January 1917 Owen had said in a letter to Susan Owen, 'I can see no excuse for deceiving you about these 4 days. I have suffered seventh hell.' The idea that the front was hell became so commonplace as to lose almost all metaphorical force, but Owen's 'seventh hell' is more precise, suggesting the concentric circles of Dante's inferno. The thought that Dante is concerned with sinners complicates the possible allusion, but usefully hints at that complex of guilt and uncertainty which marks Owen's response to religion in his poems and letters of the war.

Owen's realisation of the conditions of war and the possible significance of these conditions was powerfully and properly sensory. This leads him to relate religion and conditions in Bunyan's terms; whereby No Man's Land is like 'the eternal place of gnashing of teeth; the Slough of Despond could be contained in one of its crater-holes'. Such conditions create a Waste Land: 'We were marooned on a frozen desert, There is not a sign of life on the horizon. . . '; 'Not a blade of grass, not an insect. . . ' (from the letter to Susan Owen, 1917).

It is such hideousness that 'saps the "soldierly spirit" ' – but it is also that which puts such pressure (for Owen) on belief, and which sweeps chivalric concepts away. In poetry and letters alike the pressure fractures belief in institutionalised Christianity, which is not to say that Owen becomes a non-believer. He never achieves that sort of certainty; the evidence suggesting flux and bewilderment rather than any solid state, either of belief or of atheism.

It is, I think, fair to say that Owen, understandably, even honourably, never established a theology in his writings of the war. All he is able to do is to ask questions and express doubts. So he contemplates 'one of Christ's essential commands' as being 'Passivity at any price! . . . be killed; but do not kill', and, in the same letter, places Christ in No Man's Land, where 'men often hear His voice'. This is the letter of May 1917 which also contains the famous question 'And am I not myself a conscientious objector with a very seared conscience?'. But a soldier is in the killing business, is implicated so long as he goes on serving, as Owen himself did, and so the uncertainties of 'At a Calvary . . . ' recur. There may be suggestions of a new vision, like the 'I, too, saw God through mud' of 'Apolgia pro Poemata Meo', but these are moments, undeveloped, enigmatic, incomplete. There are clear accounts of disobedience to God's precepts, as in the retelling of the parable of Abraham and Isaac. In Owen's version ('The Parable of the Old Man and the Young') Abraham disobeys God's command:

> But the old man . . . slew his son,
> And half the seed of Europe, one by one.

The poem's old man suggests the generational theme of much of the disillusioned verse of the war, the fathers of poems like Owen's own 'S.I.W.' who would sooner see sons 'dead than in disgrace', or the Sassoon generals who mastermind massacres. There is also the heresy of 'Soldier's Dream'. Here 'kind Jesus' works to frustrate the war by fouling its machinery. 'But God was vexed, and gave all power to Michael;/And when I woke he'd seen to our repairs'. This is an ironic reworking of Milton's *Paradise Lost*, but the casual tone ('kind Jesus', 'pikel/Michael') hints at a self-protective defensiveness, almost a doubt as to whether even heresy is worthwhile. In 'Exposure' God's entrance into the poem is marked by ambiguity; in 'The Show' the capitalised 'He' is Death, in a context which calls for God; in 'Futility' God is an absent presence. 'Spring Offensive', which belongs to the last few weeks of Owen's life, underlines the passing of the chivalric ('No alarms/Of bugles, no high flags, no clamorous haste') and, as the offensive gains in Spring momentum, 'the whole sky burned/With fury against them'. This sense of a hostile cosmos is checked for a moment by 'Some say God caught them even before they fell', but this tentative suggestion is itself questioned in the last verse paragraph.

In 'Some say God caught them' Owen seems to have little doubt that if God troubles to catch anyone, it is the soldier who deserves to be caught and saved. If there is, for Owen, anything to be made of Christ in the experience of this war it is the idea of Christ with/as soldier. This can, in turn, be linked with Owen's expressed motives for returning to the Front, where he hoped to serve this concept of Christ by serving the soldiers. Owen thus becomes, in part, a Christ-figure (by serving the soldiers) and, in part, a Mary Magdalene (by serving Christ). The ambiguity seems appropriate, for Owen does not resolve the uncertainties of 'At a Calvary. . . '. I suspect that he was most powerfully drawn not to ethereality but to the 'warm live hand' of 'Maundy Thursday'. But, beyond this, lurks the issue of whether Owen's failure to resolve ambiguities tells us more about him than about Christianity – or vice versa.

## NOTES

1. Trotter (ed.), *Valour and Vision*, p. 75.
2. Respectively, Reilly, p. 122; Tulloch, p. 191; Trotter, p. 12; Clarke, p. 246.
3. Dobell, pp. 12, 37.
4. 'Ten Hundred Thousand Strong', Tulloch, p. 66.
5. Respectively, 'The Volunteer', Parsons, p. 41; 'England to her Sons', Gardner, p. 10; *More Songs*. . . , p. 131; Hibberd/Onions, p. 168. 'The Volunteer' and 'England to her Sons' were written by these volunteers shortly before the outbreak of war.
6. *The Best of Fragments from France*, ed. T. and V. Holt, Milestone, 1978, p. 17.
7. Trotter, p. 145.
8. See n.2, Clarke.
9. *The Great War and Modern Memory* (1975), Oxford, 1979, p. 118.
10. Trotter, pp. 52, 119.
11. P. MacGill, *Soldier Songs*, Jenkins, 1917, p. 113.
12. J.M. Read, *Atrocity Propaganda*, Yale, 1941, pp. 41–2.
13. Reilly, p. 140.
14. Respectively, ibid. pp. 127, 115, 104.
15. Clarke, p. 47.
16. *The Unutterable Beauty*, p. 24.
17. *Collected Poems*, Allen and Unwin (1929), 1933, p. 84.
18. *The War Poems*, p. 24.
19. Hibberd/Onions, p. 98.
20. Quoted in *The Collected Poems*. . . , ed. E. Blunden, Chatto and Windus, 1963, p. 23.
21. *Collected Poems*, Faber, 1956, p. 50.
22. J. Wood (ed.) *A Life Well Lived*. . . , Partridge, n.d., p. 94.
23. *The New Elizabethans*, p. 16.
24. *Gloucestershire Friends*, Sidgwick and Jackson, 1917, p. 34.
25. ibid., p. 69.
26. *War Poems*, p. 16.
27. *War Poems and Others*, p. 95. All quotations in this section are from this edition.

# 6

# ENGLAND – COUNTRY AND HISTORY

One way of seeing the coming of the Great War is as the triumph of nationalism over internationalism. It had been argued that a major war was impossible, either because business had become international to the point where national economies could not sustain a war, or because worker internationalism would lead the masses to refuse to fight each other. Obviously, both views were wrong. Even while such arguments were being advanced, nationalism was alive and well, to be sharpened by propaganda as soon as the war began. Propaganda works by blackening your enemies and by simultaneously projecting a view of your own nation as morally worthy. History (usually pseudo-history) is used to reinforce the nationalistic stereotypes of propaganda. Most of the verse to be considered in this chapter is propaganda, in the sense that it displays stereotypical images of the nation to reinforce the 'need' for the war. It uses, of necessity, extreme selection and the power of myth.

The basic vision, so far as England is concerned, is of a rural country; more specifically, a terrain which suggests the south of England. So, when Noel Corbett, in 'Lines written somewhere in the North Sea', speaks of the homeland, it is of 'little red-roofed villages/That nestle close in some deep crease amid the rolling wealds'.[1] The landscape is 'flecked with sheep' and the corn is 'standing deep above the ripening fields'. The 'England that we know' is a land of 'fruitful fields and purling streams', inevitably 'sea-girt' – and this is the England to die for. The blend is important, with its intimations of Shakespeare and Keats and with its stress on an almost maternal security. When, in 1914, John Freeman suggests that England is happy 'in the brave that die/For wrongs not hers', his England nods to towns, but surrounds them with the rural:

> Happy in all her dark woods, green fields, towns,
> Her hills and rivers and her chafing sea.[2]

This bucolic sanitising is repeated by John Galsworthy, in his recruiting poem 'England to Free Men':

> From misty hill and misty fen,
> From cot, and town, and plough and moor,
> Come in. . . .[3]

Here again 'town' is literally surrounded by country.

Such visions seek to suppress both the fact that England was now, as for some decades, an urban industrial country and actualities of rural labouring lives. Corbett's cosiness (almost a kind of infantilism) further marginalises climate and the more rugged, sometimes bleak, landscapes of the midlands and north. These visions are at once both pseudo-historical and mythical, invoking the centuries when England was a rural country and transforming the landscape into pure pastoral forms. Some specificity, albeit very limited, is called for to convey reality in these terms, but a number of poets avoid even Corbett's thin detailing and use the word 'England' as merely a reference point for moral values.

It is significant that 'history' facilitates the elision of Britain into England (and vice versa) since this allows poets to exploit both pasts. Bertram Dobell provides a good example of how this works as propaganda. He uses dichotomies, in terms of which Germans are feudal, tyrannic, barbarous and shifty; while to be British is to be 'free-born', chivalric, honourable and trusty; and he gains his effects by repetition of such loaded references as those to Attila. Laurence Binyon also associates national heritage with freedom. He avoids detail completely, so that a poem like 'The Fourth of August' becomes merely a chant.[4] C.A. Alington, as late as 1918, presents the English dead as responding to country as a trustworthy mother, instinctively associated with unity, freedom and the right.[5] Such 'sovereign pride of race' is offered by W.M.L. Hutchinson as allowing the 'English Mother' to match the Spartan mother of legend: 'Take, England, this my son, for he is thine'.[6] Such poems lack anything that could be called analysis. Their potency is in their imprecise evocations, but they cannot be dismissed as incompetent. Skill is utilised to serve cause and country. In *The Times* for All Souls Day, 1916, Beatrix Brice (Miller) anonymously honours the BEF as the vanguard:

Oh, little mighty Force, your way is ours,
This land inviolate your monument.[7]

Unity of effort and a vague invocation of sea-girt England will memorialise the BEF's dead, the effect subliminally reinforced by the idea of the country as a woman protected from rape (this carrying chivalric overtones), while the grim fact of death is elevated /displaced to 'monument'. Such writing skilfully, if perhaps unconsciously, makes use of atavistic fossils of nationalism.

When Hutchinson invokes Sparta, when Alington sees England as mother, and when Corbett renders the home country as rural memory, they are – in a very broad sense – calling upon either history or metonymy or both. They are seeking to contain the war within patterns of value which give it purpose and dignity, through a sacrifice which is in defence of something worth defending – mother or 'red-roofed villages'. But there is another important icon which is socially revealing: school or college. So Alexander Robertson (missing in July 1916) writes 'A Dream of New College', in which, having summoned 'a College garden in the shade' and the 'time-unravaged' beauty 'near these towers', he presents the college as, in effect, that for which the war is being fought. Men die 'Glad that the men of future days might see/Inviolate this beauty's sanctity'. New College, with 'the gardens old', is 'An emblem of all beauty' – or will be if 'the soul/Of England shall escape a cursed control'. The vision is of a faintly pastoral, sacred and ancient England epitomised; and it is, it seems, this for which men are fighting. Even if, as seems unlikely, this idea occurred to many rankers, there is the thought that it should not be encouraged. More simply, J.M. Rose-Troup recalls Henry Newbolt, in 1916. Sons of Harrow 'will follow up and play the game'. Those who have done this have 'fought for England' and 'Kept Harrow's honour spotless', but the assimilation of the one to the other is marked by the final line: 'We live, we fight, we die for Harrow's sake', whereby it would appear that Harrow epitomises England (which is ridiculous) or that England exists to sustain Harrow (which is preposterous). Charles Scott-Moncrieff can accommodate 'vile death' in a context which is 'Mud-stained and rain-sodden, a sport for flies and lice' by suggesting that this will make possible the continued sustenance of seeing 'Windsor Castle towering on the crest/And Eton still enshrined among remembering trees'.[8] Such possible preservation allows the victims of war to die 'radiant'; will serve Englishmen who leave 'city cares behind' to experience renewed 'boyish ardour' in face of a monarch's castle and a sacred public school. Scott-Moncrieff uses sonnet form competently enough for a collocation of potent images to work persuasively – radiant, city, boyish, Windsor, Eton, enshrined, trees – but, of course, there are readings which, deconstructing, would react against the persuasion, picking up the threatening overtones of 'towering', questioning the justice of what is sacred about Eton, feeling excluded by the glib sexism of the lines.

Robertson's 'time-ravaged beauty', reminiscent of Keats's 'still unravished bride' ('Ode on a Grecian Urn') can be linked with ideas of an England which is unchanging, ancient and a repository of an enduring, cyclic spiritual history. The past is seen in terms of 'epiphanies' rendered in a talismanic name-chant. The names reach back as far as Arthurian myth when Maurice Baring invokes 'Knights of the Table Round . . . Lancelot and Tristram' to place Lord Lucas ('killed November 3, 1916') in a paradise of heroes,[9] but the most common device is to call up the spirits of great battles and great leaders. For the patrician Herbert Asquith, the clerkly volunteer 'goes to join the men of Agincourt',[10] while sergeant Joseph Lee of the Black Watch recalls Drake and the Armada, Wellington and Waterloo, to place the combatants of the First World War in a glorious tradition:

> Our steel's as true, brave boys,
> Our blood's as blue, brave, bully boys,
> And Britain trusts to me and you!
>
> ('When the Armada. . .')

Lee also draws on a more personal continuity in '1815–1915' by addressing that poem 'To my grandfather who fought at Waterloo', the present war being seen as a new Waterloo.[11] The most elaborate version of this type of allusion which I have come across, however, is a long poem, 'The Old Way', by Ronald Hopwood, which draws on Newbolt, Masefield and Kipling. The poem uses Nelson, Hawke, Howard and 'Gloriana' to answer the rhetorical question as to whether or not things have changed. Not only has there been no vital change, but the glories of the past provide sustenance and strength: 'I know it often helped to think of you', and 'See the sober grey is shining like Tudor green and gold!'. Gordon Alchin's 'The Road' draws on the resistance to Roman legions and Norman armies to give 'proof to any close observer,/That men are little changed today!'. His poems ends

What matter cannon, petrol, piston?
The *men* are just the same to-day![12]

Alchin is using the idea of an Englishness (first British-Arthurian, then Saxon-Hereward) which endures and finally triumphs. His poem marginalises the *success* of the Roman and Norman invasions, ignores the blood-contributions such invaders have made to the English race, and stresses 'spirit' at technology's expense. It is assured, but absurd.

A common feature of the various invocations surveyed here is that they make history out of historico-mythic moments. 'Nelson', for example, is made almost as mythic as Lancelot, and 'Agincourt' is an icon of English military victory against the odds, as is 'Armada'. The symbols, however, only work in this poetry so long as they are allowed to remain myth: they lose potency as soon as the advantages the English had at Agincourt are remembered, or when the weather is brought to bear on the episode of the Armada. Similarly, there is plenty in the social and familial habits and attitudes relevant to English public schools which would undercut the image of Eton, as would remembering how much justice Hardy's Jude embodies in relation to ancient English universities. The cunning or innocent deployment of such symbols in this poetry makes it clearly pro-pagandist, chauvinist and dangerous; yet, at the same time, the symbols must be seen as consolations to those who are caught in their web. For such, the experience of the 'flies and lice' may be made not just bearable, but ultimately glorious. How far this consolation worked in the psyches of its proponents is hard to say. If we understand Corbett's England in terms of a return to the womb and link this with the enduring infantilism of the public school tradition, we have a nexus which some of us would see as an important national disability. It may be fair to add that the regression is understandable in the context of the Great War, but it remains a clear indication of the restricted range of such poets as have been quoted. It is difficult to see what meaning their articulations could have for a Clydeside shipworker or a Welsh miner. Also, it should be emphasised that the implications of 'England is fighting for Eton' are both silly and offensive in relation to most people, marginalising the vast majority of the population. There is, however, the further thought that the social history of the twentieth century suggests that, in the final analysis, this was perhaps what was being fought for – the protection of the privileges of the few.

Broadly speaking, the poetry of the First World War which moves away from glorification of such 'Englishness' did not incorporate a revisionist view of history or of ideas of England; at least not directly. But there are a few poems which make use of a grimmer idea of the past than those we have so far been concerned with. E.A. Mackintosh, for example, had a privileged education, but works free of the images dealt with above. The regiments he imagines in 'Before the Summer' ('1916, before the Somme battle') are 'broken' and 'come stumbling down the line', leaving their dead 'Between the battered trenches'. The conclusion is that it is better to die than to live with such memories:

> God grant we too be lying there in wind and mud and rain
> Before the broken regiments come stumbling back again.

In 'Cha Til Maccruimein', however, this bleak view is related to history.[13] The poet-voice hears 'a lonely pibroch/Out of an older war', but its message is simply the dirge 'MacCrimmon comes no more'. The poet-figure's friends march out to die; they dream of 'honour and wealth to come', but the poet hears only 'a woman singing' that MacCrimmon no longer comes. In the final stanza 'The grey old ghosts of the ancient fighters' are headed by MacCrimmon, whose tune is 'weary and sore':

> 'On the gathering day, for ever and ever,
> MacCrimmon comes no more'.

The sense these poems give is that Mackintosh's English education at St Paul's and Oxford has given way before the pressures of war experience. As we have seen (see page 57) Mackintosh was gassed on the Somme before being killed at Cambrai in 1917: the dirge from Scottish history seems more apt than the pastoralism seen earlier.

In contrast to Mackintosh, W.W. Gibson, as noted above (see page 73) seems not to have served abroad and yet his 1916 volume *Battle* is one of the more interesting early attempts at a response which is other than blank acceptance of the war. His poem 'Comrades', from that volume, uses the tight forms and stylish flatness of the Georgians, and it refers to Waterloo - but only to remind the soldier imagined as marching in Flanders of death:

> 'Once too I marched in Flanders,
>   The very spit of you,
> And just a hundred years since,

To fall at Waterloo . . .
To the ending of the day's march
I'll bear you company.[14]

As with Mackintosh, a revenant brings only a grim reminder.

None of those poets who are usually considered the major voices of the war has so far been discussed in this chapter, and for the excellent reason that they largely avoid the attitudes we have been considering. The past in Owen's poetry is mainly religious and literary (although rural England is ambiguously invoked in the bugles 'from sad shires' of 'Anthem for Doomed Youth'), while for Sassoon the past is mainly the immediately older generation and must be attacked. Neither Rosenberg nor Gurney is nationalistic. None of the four finds pattern or consolation in Agincourt or the Armada, Waterloo or Trafalgar, New College or Harrow.

Yet what these poets represent is not a repudiation of ideas of the past and the country, but a different set of attitudes to such ideas. Both the title and verse-form of Owen's '1914' suggest Brooke, and the poem embodies a cyclic view of history (or, at least, the need for such a view). The Sassoon of 'Absolution' (April–Summer 1915) is also close to Brooke, while Gurney dedicated his 'Sonnets 1917' to his memory. But each of these poets comes to be aware that the symbols of past glory and the pastoral view of country are inadequate for experiences of this war.

Sassoon is famous partly because of the prose memoirs of 'George Sherston', and, in the first volume, *Memoirs of a Fox-Hunting Man*, he produced the classic account of the immediate pre-war years as Golden Idyll. His own experiences before 1914 are artfully shaped to create a Sherston who is a happy barbarian of the shires. Part eight ends with a remark about 'my callow comprehension of terrestrial affairs', while part nine ('In the Army') opens with Sherston ruminating 'on my five weeks' service' as a trooper.[15] There is a phasing into war experience, but Sassoon is determined to achieve a sharp contrast between war and pre-war. *Fox-Hunting Man* was first published in 1928, whereas most of Sassoon's poems of the war belong to 1915–18. But these poems focus upon the present with a fierceness that has little time for history, except in so far as recent history has made the 'scarlet Majors at the Base' of 'Base Details' and the bishop of ' "They" '. Sassoon's view of this immediate past has the same edge as Richard Aldington's in *Death of a Hero*, and it is a view which also defines England as Home. But in the place of sacrificing mothers and sustaining castles and colleges, there are music hall and Parliament, which the poet of ' "Blighters" ' and 'Fight to a Finish' wishes to obliterate. There is nothing in England or its history to sustain. George Sherston turns away from his pastoral past; the poet of Sassoon's war poems cuts himself off from his immediate ancestors.

Owen is less of a satirist, but he focuses, like Sassoon, upon the present. So far as the nation is concerned, it is for Owen mainly interesting for its poets, and particularly for the English Romantics. Symbols of nationalistic pride mean nothing to Owen, while the implications of his concentration upon trench experience are that the only worthwhile contemporary England is there. Isaac Rosenberg, unsurprisingly, since he was an East End Jew of recent east European origin, has little sense of England and its past. His major poems of the war hardly use the word which runs like a thread through so many poems by others (although 'The Dead Heroes' of 1915 does have 'Their blood is England's heart;/By their dead hands/It is their noble part/That England stands'). Religious myth and Jewish history displace ideas of England in Rosenberg's work, providing a tougher, more credible sustenance than 'official' Nelson or Waterloo could. When England is named in 'Break of Day. . . ', it is to make a point about the rat's indifference to nationality, and when great military heroes of the past are invoked they are 'Napoleon and Caesar' (Frenchman, Roman), not Wellington or Nelson. Moreover, in the poem in question ('Soldier: Twentieth Century') the leadership principle stressed in the type of history that proceeds by listing great names is replaced by the 'great new Titan', who is the suffering ranker 'That has outgrown the pallid days,/ When you slept like Circe's swine'.[10] This is a striking reworking of Brooke's theme of awakening from inertia, and it is given edge by remembering that the Titans were rebels against tyranny. The contrast can be put another way. Rosenberg's sense of Jewish history and its closeness to his own experience ('Moses, from whose loins I spring' – 'The Jew') means that the war is hardly a surprise, either as a general fact or a particular experience. It is this, I think, that encourages that seeming objectivity of his best verse – there is nothing surprising about the horrors of 'Dead Man's Dump':

> Earth has waited for them,
> All the time of their growth

Fretting for their decay. . . .[17]

Blood and ravaging are parts of what Rosenberg culturally and socially knows – quite apart from the war. Sassoon (also Jewish) had more to learn, while the poets who were, it seems, sustained by rural England, school as mother, and heroic icons could not bear to learn or did not live long enough.

For Edmund Blunden, the war is a violation of history, and part of that history is English. Blunden is often remembered as a pastoralist and as a mourner for the war's destruction of landscapes and buildings. The famous 'harmless young shepherd in a soldier's coat' who is the author-figure of *Undertones of War* is a device to facilitate 'innocent' recording of war experience and also a defence mechanism; but the figure can also be seen as a living reminder of what, in Blunden's terms, the war threatens to destroy.

Blunden's effort, in poems and memoir alike, is, in fact, to keep the 'harmless young shepherd' alive. It is his conviction that this past – of shepherds, fine buildings and nature – is valuable that sustains him; and the (pastoral) literature of this tradition is an important part of this sustaining. 'Vlamertinghe: Passing the Chateau, July, 1917' opens by quoting and alluding to Keats:

'And all her silken flanks with garlands drest' –
But if you ask me, mate, the choice of colour
Is scarcely right; this red should have been duller.

How unsettled and unsettling the struggle can be is clear in 'Another Journey from Béthune to Cuinchy', where one version of the poet-figure (the war-realist) comments upon another (the Romantic):

I see him walking
In a golden-green ground,
Where pink faced babies
And skylarks abound;
But that's his own business.
My time for trench round.

But although it seems clear that Blunden loves 'England' and that his England is a pastoral myth, two important qualifications need to be made. One is that Blunden's descriptions of the rural world are not pastoral in the sense of being made up of a tissue of stereotypical references. They are certainly literary, but they have detail and richness of observation, suggesting Thompson's *The Seasons* rather than Elizabethan lyric. The second point is perhaps the more important – that Blunden's nature is not chauvinistic. The sense given is that for him (as for Edward Thomas) it is natural to love English nature because that is his heritage. This does not necessitate a sense of superiority, and Blunden responds to Belgian and French nature as readily as to English. When Blunden writes 'Gouzeaucourt' and 'The Prophet' the foreign landscapes are not valued because they recall England. 'Rural Economy' has no place names:[18] Blunden is an internationalist of the country.

But perhaps the most interesting figure is, once again, Ivor Gurney. Like his friend and fellow-poet, F.W. Harvey, Gurney was deeply embedded in Gloucestershire, and Gurney was also fascinated by the past, his identifications with figures from history issuing, in his madness, in the conviction that he spoke with and in the voice of such figures. Gurney's two volumes of the war period are shot through with love of his country:

> God, that I might see
>     Framilode once again!
> Redmarley, all renewed,
>     Clear shining after rain.
> And Cranham, Cranham trees. . . .
>
> ('The Fire Kindled')

> thoughts of Gloucester filled us –
> Roads against windy skies
> At sunset, Severn river,
> Red inn-blinds, country cries.
>
> ('Toasts and Memories')

Gurney's England readily becomes Gloucestershire, and can be seen as Mother, to be 'served' by the soldier ('Strange Service'). Elsewhere, though, in these volumes Gurney comes closer to Brooke:

> If it were not for England, who would bear
> This heavy servitude one moment more?
>
> ('Servitude')

> We have done our utmost, England, terrible
> And dear taskmistress, darling Mother and stern.
>
> ('England the Mother')[19]

The titles of these two volumes ('Severn and Somme', 'War's Embers') suggest that they represent Gurney as War Poet. They do so, accurately, in the sense that they indicate what Gurney was writing while serving at the Front. But this conceals the fact that the majority of Gurney's most important poems about the war were written after it was over, and the further point that Gurney must be seen either as not primarily a War Poet or as a poet of the war even when he is not writing directly about it. He is perhaps best seen, like Edward Thomas, as a great poet for whom the war was a fundamental experience. In France, sights bring memories of home, but so do the voices of comrades; and Gurney can render the great yearning for home:

> being sick of body and heart,
> Too sick for anything but hoping that all might depart –
> We back in England again, and white roads to walk on. . . .
> > ('Riez Bailleul' – 'Behind the line. . . ')

But if aspects of the war recall England, this process can also be reversed:

> It was after war; Edward Thomas had fallen at Arras –
> I was walking by Gloucester musing on such things
> As fill his verse with goodness; it was February; the long house
> Straw-thatched of the mangels stretched two wide wings;
> And looked as part of the earth heaped up by dead soldiers. . . .
> > ('The Mangel-Bury')

Gurney is considered more closely in another chapter. The point I want to make here is that England and history are active sustainings in his poetry, in a way which is far richer than the dehistoricised symbols discussed earlier. This vitality can be seen in a variety of ways. It is there in the natural manner in which Gurney writes of retiring to 'The warm room . . . Where my music waits, and O/Ben Jonson lies . . . To delight my man's nature with his great spirit' ('Snow'): Gurney earns the right to speak of such figures of the past as 'Many my good friends' ('To Clare'). This is underlined by how, for Gurney, country lives in the voices of comrades at the Front – like the 'Infinite lovely chatter of Bucks accent' in 'The Silent One'. Past and country live for Gurney, because they become one with the present. This is seen again in his sense of the landscape as written on by the past. So Gurney can speak with conviction of 'My friends of Greece or Rome, Cotswold, my two thousand years' home' ('The Noble Wars of Troy'). When he seeks the 'spirit' of England, it is in the nature of his landscape, but this is no pastoral vision or etiolate dream. Instead it has the tangibility of John Clare:

> If England, her spirit lives anywhere

> It is by Severn, by hawthorns and grand willows
> Earth heaves up twice a hundred feet in air
> And ruddy clay-falls scooped out to the weedy shallows.[20]

As suggested in passing above, Gurney and Edward Thomas have things in common. Thomas is almost exclusively a poet of the country, but in a very particular sense. He is not a patriotic poet, nor is he a pastoralist, in the usual sense of that term. 'Country' in Thomas has almost the old meaning of 'my county', although this usually meant something like 'my county' and Thomas is not the poet of a single county. The kind of country conveyed by Thomas's poetry (and prose) is something that has been possessed, although the idea of possession here has little to do with property or ownership: he is not the poet of country house or of enclosure as a means of asserting property rights. 'Possession' in these poems is a way of knowing the countryside, of making it part of self, and it is acquired by walking. 'The Owl' begins

> Downhill I came, hungry, and yet not starved;
> Cold, yet had heat within me. . . .
> . . . . . . . . . . .
> Then at the inn I had food, fire, and rest. . . .

Inns are the resting places of itinerants (or at least of those with some money), and Thomas's personae are walkers, although this is often implied rather than directly stated, a matter of the attention given to paths and of the close observation which only walking brings ('First known when lost'). Usually, too, the encounters in Thomas's poems are with humble labourers and/or itinerants. I am thinking, for example, of the face of Lob (' – rough, brown, sweet as any nut – a land face, sea-blue-eyed') and of the ploughman of 'As the Team's Head Brass'. The poem 'Roads' suggests that it is the durability and variety of roads which attract Thomas:

> Roads go on
> While we forget. . . .
> . . . . . . . . .
> The next turn may reveal
> Heaven: upon the crest
> The close pine clump, at rest
> And black, may Hell conceal.
> . . . . . . . . . .
> Often footsore, never
> Yet of the road I weary. . . .

'The close pine clump' makes a point about the specificity of Thomas, for, wherever his line of thought is tending, observation of the physical continues:

The waters running frizzled over gravel

('The Brook')

The shell of a little snail bleached
In the grass; chip of flint, and mite
Of chalk. . . .

('But these things also')

This is one of the things which links Thomas with Gurney, and both with Clare.

Thomas is so specific that it is impossible for his poetry to have a Brookean sense of England. The type of 'thinking' that sees the nation epitomised in Eton or Clifton is absent, partly because a search for epitomes in Thomas leads to Lob or a bunch of nettles, and partly because Thomas's verse works away from such abstractions:

They have taken the gable from the roof of clay
On the long swede pile. They have let in the sun
To the white, and gold and purple of curled fronds
Unsunned. . . .

('Swedes')

Thomas's love of England (if that is not itself too abstract) is of possessed parts and of the land he happens to belong to:

She is all we know and live by, and we trust
She is good and must ensure, loving her so. . . .

('This is no Case . . . ')[21]

Although the logic of this poem leads from these lines to the final 'And as we love ourselves we hate her foe', the same logic allows an enemy the same right to the same viewpoint. That patriotism which is based on a sense of superiority is absent.

The figure of Lob has already been mentioned. The perspective of Thomas's poems is usually solitary and the encounters within poems are usually between single figures. The itnerant is a common feature, passing along roads or paths on foot. Lob is a kind of summary, with an ancestry so deep in history as to fade easily into legend. Lob *is* a history, an alternative to that of houses and parks, schools and colleges - and this history is of the outsider and the unprivileged, of footpaths as against walls and forest as against gardens. This should be enough to make the point that we should not expect Thomas's poetry to show any sense of England as something defined by relation to other countries. Thomas's England is defined *within* the geographical boundaries of the country, in terms of observed, possessed specific experiences.

Thomas enlisted in the Artists' Rifles in July 1915, and volunteered for service overseas in December 1916. He left Le Havre for the Front Line in February 1917 and was killed at the beginning of the Arras offensive on 9 April. There was thus very little time for Thomas to adjust to the direct experience of war, and his last poem was written before he embarked from Southampton. So his few weeks in France are a poetic blank, and in that sense his imagination did not make an adjustment from Home to Front. This observation, however, leads to the thought that a poet who depended so much on absorbed particulars could only adjust to radically new contexts if given more time than Thomas, sadly, had. Moreover, the steeping in specificity which is of the essence of Thomas's gift ensures that his is a poetry set against both nationalism and war because it cannot readily have the generalised vision endemic to such concepts. Other nations are scarcely mentioned in Thomas's poems, while overtly political themes are absent. Thomas, one might say, went to war with no ready-made pen with which to write about it.

Yet it will not do to explain the lack of self-evident war poems in Thomas's output by pointing to the brevity of his time in France. He lived until April 1917 and the war had involved England from its start, preoccupying many who never crossed the channel. What needs to be faced in Thomas is an absorbing of the attention by the specifics of his 'country', which, at least superficially, marginalises the war. This leaves him open to charges of complacency and indifference, similar to those which have been made against Jane Austen. It also leads to the view that Thomas is not a war poet at all. If, however, we attend to how the poetry as a whole works, it becomes clear that Thomas has a special contribution to make in the context of war. In summary, the point is that Thomas's verse argues the case for attention to an historico-present England which is further threatened by the war.

R.George Thomas's edition prints 144 poems by Edward Thomas, the earliest belonging to November/December 1914, the latest dated 13 January 1917. They all, therefore, come within the timespan of the war. By my count only fifteen of these poems, at most, allude to the war, some briefly and/or obliquely; and the allusions come almost invariably in the context of Home. 'Man and Dog' is typical. It is a poem of forty-eight lines and the old man is a characteristic Thomas figure, an itinerant worker of 'hoeing and harvesting/In half the shires where corn and couch will grow'. Immediately after this (ll. 18–19) we learn that

> His sons, three sons, were fighting, but the hoe
> And reap-hook he lik'd, or anything to do with trees.

Later, the old man comments:

> 'Many a man sleeps worse tonight
> Than I shall'. 'In the trenches?'. 'Yes, that's right.
> But they'll be out of that – I hope they be –
> This weather, marching after the enemy'.

(ll. 39–42)

What is important here is how the war is recognised. First, it is personal: the old man's sons are fighting. Second, the war is not, it seems, his chief object of interest ('but the hoe/And reap-hook he lik'd'). Third, there is the capacity for concern for others. The poem ends with a typical Thomas separation:

> They passed,
> The robin till the next day, the man for good,
> Together in the twilight of the wood.

Thomas registers the impact of the war in the crannies; and this says 'even here' as well as 'only to this degree'. But the latter can easily be underestimated, as 'As the Team's Head Brass' makes clear. There the way in which the war has interrupted the agricultural cycle is a significant instance of the ramifications of the conflict. The interlocutor asks the ploughman about the fallen elm: 'When will they take it away?', and the answer is 'When the war's over'. The longer the war, the greater the disruption; and some were wondering if it would ever end.

This, if you like, is Thomas 'getting it into proportion'. The war directly informs only some half-dozen lines of 'Man and Dog'. In 'Fifty Faggots' the poet-figure considers that before the faggots have all been burned 'The war will have ended'. In 'Wind and Mist' the dearness of the 'angled fields/Or grass and grain bounded by oak and thorn' is measured by the thought that

> Had we with Germany
> To play upon this board it could not be
> More dear than April has made it with a smile.

In such examples, the war is certainly marginalised, but this marks its ubiquity as well as its limits. It surfaces, or catches the corner of the eye; and it threatens what Thomas cares most deeply about. Moreover, Thomas is no poet of easy cleansings. His soldiers are at one with the poor and the itinerant, and the war does not transform them:

> And salted was my food, and my repose,
> Salted and sobered, too, by the bird's voice
> Speaking for all who lay under the stars,
> Soldiers and poor, unable to rejoice.

> ('The Owl')

The sons of 'Man and Dog' are the sons of an old labourer and his anonymous mate, while the men whose absence leaves the fallen elm uncleared in 'As the Team's Head Brass' are 'mates' of the ploughman. So these soldiers belong to the hard history of itinerant labour and vagrancy; to the patterns of possessed nature; and to the world of Lob. If Blunden is concerned with how the war directly destroys buildings and landscapes, Thomas registers interventions which have their origins far away, but which are damaging, potentially progressively destructive, of things far from their origins: traditions which have, for centuries, been threatened from within. For Rosenberg, the First World War seems almost to be expected, since his culture knows all too much about pogroms, diasporas and holocausts. For Thomas the war finally appears to be an extension of that which perennially threatens Lob.

There is one other important point, which is that Thomas's verse provides an oblique critique of propaganda, a critique which becomes direct in 'This is no Case. . . ':

> I hate not Germans, nor grow hot
> With love of Englishmen, to please newspapers.
> Beside my hate of one fat patriot
> My hatred of the Kaiser is love true. . . .

The war did not touch English landscapes directly to any great extent. This is not to minimalise the indirect suffering of the English people, which was enormous, but to remind the English that it was not their land which was devastated nor their citizens who were rendered refugees. Thomas communicates this indirection very precisely. Moreover, chauvinist allegations of a 'whole nation' commitment to the war need to be set against accusations from the Front of Home indifference. Thomas, it might be said, mediates between these extremes, both by his themes and by the figures he writes about:

> His sons, three sons, were fighting, but the hoe
> And reap-hook he lik'd, or anything to do with trees.

Thomas makes a valuable contribution to the response to the war in verse *because* he so rarely treats it as his subject.

## NOTES

1. Osborn, p. 88.
2. Gardner, p. 8.
3. Clarke, p. 23.
4. Trotter, p. 3.
5. 'The Trust', Trotter, p. 167.
6. 'Matri Dolorosa', Tulloch, p. 206.
7. Trotter, p. 12.
8. Osborn, pp. 190, 176, 175.
9. Trotter, p. 102.
10. Clarke, p. 153.
11. *Ballads of Battle*, pp. 57, 97.
12. Osborn, pp. 73, 45.
13. Gardner, p. 53; Osborn, p. 218.
14. p. 25.
15. Faber (1928), 1978, pp. 242–3.
16. *Collected Poems*, pp. 42, 87.
17. ibid. pp. 71, 81.
18. *Undertones of War*, pp. 267, 281, 267, 268, 258.
19. *Severn and Somme/War's Embers*, pp. 22, 66, 26, 50, 51.
20. *Collected Poems*, pp. 155, 163, 184, 185, 139.
21. *The Collected Poems. . .* , ed. R.George Thomas, Oxford, 1981. All Thomas quotations are from this edition.

# 7

# ROBERT GRAVES

For many people with some knowledge of the literature of the First World War, Robert Graves is probably remembered mainly as the author of the memoir *Goodbye to All That* (1929). Some will know that its integrity and literal truthfulness (which are not the same things) have been questioned – the former notably by Graves himself; the latter by, among others, Paul Fussell. Many will be aware of Graves as a poet some of whose poems concern the war, but readers of Graves's poems may well have seen few of these war poems, largely because Graves progressively purged his own war verse. Four early volumes – *Over the Brazier* (1916), *Goliath and David* (1916), *Fairies and Fusiliers* (1917) and *Country Sentiment* (1920) – contain most of the relevant poems, but only 'About a third of the war poems reappeared in his *Collected Poems 1914–1926* (1927)'.[1] The famous 'Recalling War' (1938) was suppressed by Graves after 1961, while 'Armistice Day, 1918' is the only war poem which appears in *Collected Poems 1975*.[2] William Graves's edition of *Poems about War* (Cassell, 1988) includes fifty-four poems, five of which had not previously been published. Although fifty-four poems is only a small fraction of Graves's total output it is a much more substantial response to the war than a single poem in the 1975 *Collected* would suggest. Graves's suppression of these poems is perhaps best seen as part of the effort to say 'goodbye to all that', yet 'A Letter from Wales' (c.1924) and 'Recalling War' suggest that this was more easily said than done. *Poems about War* obviously represents William Graves's feeling that Robert Graves's effort to clear the record should be resisted, and it has, in fact, never been entirely successful.

Graves is modestly represented in Osborn's *The Muse in Arms* (1917) and Trotter's *Valour and Vision* (1923), and the level of representation is much the same as in modern anthologies. Gardner

represents Graves at the level of Robert Nichols and Richard
Aldington; Parsons of Charles Sorley and W.W. Gibson; Black of
Nichols and Isaac Rosenberg. His position is, however, unstable,
with Graves hardly featuring in Silkin or Hussey, but in Hibberd/
Onions being represented by seven poems – only Sassoon (fourteen),
Owen (eleven) and Gurney (eight) having more. So far as criticism is
concerned, Fussell shows only passing interest in Graves as a poet of
the war; Hibberd's 1981 Macmillan Casebook *Poetry of the First
World War* has no extended discussion; Silkin is mainly interested in
Graves's relationship with Sassoon. With William Graves's *Poems
about War*, however, it is possible to see the variety and quality of
Robert Graves's achievement as a poet of the war more clearly.

Since *Poems about War* is so recent, and since it draws together the
war poems for, in effect, the first time, this volume's appearance
contributes to the case for giving a chapter to Graves in a book which
is otherwise not organised in that author-centred way. But the case
depends, essentially, on Graves's particular contribution to poetry of
the war.

Graves was 19 when, in 1914, he joined the Royal Welch Fusiliers as
a subaltern. He was the product of a public school, became a captain,
was wounded and suffered shell-shock. The profile is common
enough, but, although Graves has these experiences in common with
– among others – a number of those who wrote verse about the war,
his case is unusual. He is distinct from the majority through the
range and level of his talent, but also from the comparably talented
minority. His background is very unlike those of the plebeian
Gurney and Rosenberg; he served through the war, unlike Thomas;
he never settled to a single dominant manner, as Sassoon did; and he
survived to reflect on the war, unlike Owen. He is closest to
Blunden, another young public school man who served through the
war and contemplated it for years after, but Graves is a more varied,
more restless and experimental poet of the war than Blunden. It is
the variety of Graves's attempts to register war experience, together
with the evidence of determination to think about the war and how
to write about it, that makes his product so interesting. This product,
unevenly spanning the years 1915 to 1938, is instructive and, taken
as a whole, individual. If, as I believe, Graves is a significant poet of
the war, to be seen alongside Sassoon and Owen, Gurney and
Rosenberg, the case for giving a chapter to his war poems is partly

the effort to define his particular contribution and partly to disperse the (self-encouraged) neglect of these poems.

Two early poems from *Over the Brazier* make the point that Graves's responses to the war were never wholly conventional. 'On finding Myself a Soldier' (which Graves seems to have wanted to suppress as early as 1915) is an allegory, hardly recognisable as a war poem without its title.[3] It is Georgian in its modest, almost diminutive, language and in its use of the ABAB quatrain:

> My bud was backward to unclose,
>   A pretty baby-queen,
> Furled petal-tips of creamy rose
>   Caught in a clasp of green.

The expectation, in the second stanza, is that the unfurled bud will be 'coloured in as out', this coloration to be 'Like the flush of dawn on snow'. Instead (stanza three) this exfoliation reveals

> Twelve flamy petals ringed around
>   A heart more red than blood.

The poem is suggestive rather than precise, but the title suggests that to find yourself a soldier is to discover a maturity of violence and passion rather than of innocence and purity. The obliquity of approach and modesty of manner, amounting to diffidence in the presentation of self, are far more effective than the public grandiloquence of Rupert Brooke.

'The Shadow of Death' is yet plainer, coming close to banality, but it shows a cold-eyed recognition of war as other than trumpets and chivalric deeds. Involvement means participation in 'battle murder', and, the poem says, means also death and, with that, 'an end to my art!'. There is hyperbolic attitudinising here, but the final stanza, before lapsing into preciosity, grasps a central dilemma for the clear-sighted, anticipating Owen and Sassoon:

> To fight and kill is wrong –
>   To stay at home wronger. . . .

These are minor poems, but they strike interesting minority notes early in the war, and, in suggesting some independence of response, introduce the view that Graves is a poet who tries, in a variety of ways, to get a fix on the phenomenon which is the war.

An early example of this is to be found in the three poems which make up 'Nursery Memories'. As with 'On Finding Myself a

Soldier' the texts of these pieces do not themselves signal that they
are concerned with the war. 'Nursery Memories', as over-title,
suggests something to do with infancy, while the separate titles ('The
First Funeral', 'The Adventure', 'I Hate the Moon') are general
rather than particular. But Graves's head-notes provide the orientation, as here: 'The first corpse I saw was on the German wires, and
couldn't be buried.' William Graves prints, from Robert Graves's
own copy of *Over the Brazier*, the information that the incident on
which 'The First Funeral' is based happened at Harlech in 1899.
The poem is thus, in source, a 'nursery memory' about burying a
dead dog, and the poem's manner seeks to capture a child's way of
understanding and recording the experience:

> The whole field was so smelly;
>   We smelt the poor dog first:
> His horrid swollen belly
>   Looked just like going burst.

'The Adventure' ('Suggested by the claim of a machine-gun team to
have annihilated an enemy wire party . . . ') is 'about' a child's
game-boasting –

> To-day I killed a tiger near my shack . . .
> . . . . . . . . . . . . . . . . . . . . . . . . . . . .
> I crept up close and slung a pointed stone
> With all my might

while 'I Hate the Moon' ('After a moonlight patrol near the
Brickstacks') presents something of childhood fear and credulity:

> I *hate* the Moon and its horrible stony stare,
> And I know one day it'll do me some dreadful thing.

Here again the approach is oblique, but what is striking is
Graves's unusual angle, using – for example – a child's ability to
respond to tactile sensations to convey something of the horror of a
life lived among putrescence. Moreover, the 'nursery' perspective,
when the war-subject is centred, is suggestive: the poet is a naïve
recorder; the soldier is as a child in the grip of the war; war-
experience makes for nightmare, fear and (in a typical reorientation
of 'tunes of glory') empty boastfulness (although, of course, children
need to kill tigers to stay sane).

If, however, the 'Nursery Memories' device is seen as in part a
way of achieving a perspective which is also a distancing, a poem like

'The Dead Fox Hunter' provides quite a complex instance of Graves's individuality. There is affectionate recognition that the dead captain, who had lived 'uprightly' and died 'true', deserves heaven. For such people 'Heaven has no bars or locks, /And serves all taste'. Since this was a man who lived for hunting, 'Justice must provide' 'for him in heaven', and so

> if Heaven had no Hunt before he came,
>   Why, it must find one now . . .
> And the whole host of Seraphim complete
> Must jog in scarlet to his opening Meet.

On one level this is a comic statement of the rights of a man 'who rode straight and in hunting died'; on another it is a way of deploying humour to distance the horrors of the officer's death ('The well-known rosy colours of his face/Were almost lost in grey . . . in death/His fingers were tight-clenched between his teeth'); on another, it rewrites platitudes about heaven endorsing the war and embracing the righteous. This heaven, comically, must, in justice, establish hunting.

A final example of Graves' s restless versatility in his treatment of the war is 'To Lucasta on Going to the Wars – for the Fourth Time'. The title alludes to Richard Lovelace's poem 'To Lucasta, Going to the Warres', with its famous ending:

> I could not love thee (Deare) so much,
>   Lov'd I not Honour more.

Graves is using a poem of the English Civil War of the mid-seventeenth century to provide a perspective on the First World War, and, moreoever, a poem which, as the ending suggests, deploys the language of moral choice. But Graves's title, with its concluding words 'for the fourth time', adds a note of weary iteration, which is picked up in the text proper with Lucasta's lover returning to the front 'his fourth time, hating war' (later 'This bloody war'). The behavioural mask of this weary combatant can be seen as 'Cavalier'; he, returning,

> laughs as calmly as he can
> And flings an oath

but what sustains him is pride, not 'courage, love, or hate', and specifically the pride of being 'a Fusilier'. This pride in regiment (which is marked in *Goodbye* . . . ) is something distinct from patriotism and the causes of war, even from ethics:

> It doesn't matter what's the cause,
>   What wrong they say we're righting,
> A curse for treaties, bonds and laws . . . .

It is pride in the army unit, and thus internalised. The poem's fusilier is indifferent to the appeals of propaganda and disenchanted with war. Lovelace's 'Honour', with its chivalric overtones, has given way to the narrower 'pride' of Graves's version. Yet Graves has provided a modernisation of Lovelace's style: the laughing, swearing fusilier ('Playing at cards with Death') is a modern Cavalier and the pose is what matters, what you live for, and thus a defence mechanism.

This adaptation of Lovelace's poem is built on contrasts: between the hatred of war and pride in role-playing, and between that pride and the lack of commitment to a cause or an analysis of rights and wrongs. In this way it reflects one of the recurrent themes of Graves's war poetry: the awfulness of the war set against a positive response to aspects of involvement in it. The early 'A Dead Boche' (July 1915) is perhaps Graves's most direct account of the horrors, being in part an exercise in Sassoon's kind of reportage:

> a dead Boche; he scowled and stunk
>   With clothes and face a sodden green,
> Big-bellied, spectacled, crop-haired,
> Dribbling black blood from nose and beard.

There is no effort at sympathy here, the dead German being simply a disgusting physical presence, but although 'scowled' suggests hostility on the part of the dead man the poem registers no patriotic hatred. Both title and text use the term 'Boche', which is often one of contempt or hatred, but here it is no more than part of what is loathsome to the senses. The corpse is part of the war, becomes a metonymy for it. More specifically, it is offered as the antidote to 'songs . . . of blood and fame':

> To-day I found in Mametz Wood
> A certain cure for lust of blood.

Obviously, this 'cure' is powerfully physical, incorporated in the decaying flesh and putrid smell of the corpse, and there is no suggestion that the corpse is like this because it is a German one. As the foul detail fills the second stanza physical items marginalise everything else. Arguments about the causes of the war, or its rights and wrongs, are not even – as in 'To Lucasta . . . ' – mentioned, the suggestion being that the 'cure' renders such considerations no longer relevant. Such a perception, if insufficient, is nevertheless an important first step to the abolition of war.

'A Dead Boche' marks one of Graves's sane certainties – that war is filth. But this ground rule does not prevent recognition that, in war, moral good may operate or be developed. 'Two Fusiliers' (Graves's pride in regiment has more in common with professional soldiers like Joseph Lee than with amateurs) is a poem about comradeship, and comradeship is often stressed by writers about the war as being the greatest gift to come from the experience. Graves works to restrain idealism and/or grandiloquence by specifying the details which have constructed the comradeship:

> By wire and wood and stake we're bound,
> By Fricourt and by Festubert,
> By whipping rain, by the sun's glare,
> By all the misery and loud sound . . . .

This gives a degree of precision to the claims of the last lines:

> By Death: we faced him, and we found
> Beauty in Death,
> In dead men, breath.

Even if a reader feels, as I do, that these lines suppress what 'A Dead Boche' suggests about war death, we are left with a strong sense of a bonding which is to be valued. This comradeship informs the vision of the future in 'Familiar Letter to Siegfried Sassoon' ('From Bivouacs at Mametz Wood, July 13th, 1916'). This poem, belonging to the tradition of the verse epistle, again illustrates Graves's versatility and his assurance as a 'professional' poet, confidently handling his octosyllabic couplets to create a relaxed intimacy that reaches back in English literary history at least as far as Thomas Wyatt. It is a poem about recuperation –

> In Gweithdy Bach we'll rest a while,
> We'll dress our wounds and learn to smile
> With easier lips

– but the purpose of this is made clear enough:

> Until we feel a match once more
> For *anything* but another war.

During the war leave and 'rest and recreation' were – from the army's point of view – fundamentally designed to prepare soldiers for the return to the front. Graves's lines are in a sense a sardonic commentary on this. The poem, however, is primarily a vision of the life Graves and Sassoon may lead 'when it's over', a life which is to include Sassoon being introduced to the topography and myth of Graves's landscape, the mutual writing of poetry, the resting mentioned above, and travelling together:

> So then we'll kiss our families,
> And sail away across the seas. . . .

The poem ends with the exotic and with art:

> Perhaps eventually we'll get
> Among the Tartars of Thibet,
> Hobnobbing with the Chungs and Mings,
> And doing wild, tremendous things
> In free adventure, quest and fight,
> And God! what poetry we'll write!

The light, almost playful tone catches quite beautifully the sense that this is a fantasy 'From Bivouacs at Mametz Wood', but 'Two Fusiliers' has it that such locations breed the comradeship from which such a fantasy can come. Also, the lightness of tone should not lead us to ignore where this comradeship tends: the friends will leave their families, travelling far from them and (so far as the poem is concerned) ending up well away from home. The poem is an attractive celebration of comradeship, but it does carry intimations of exile. Gweithdy Bach is represented as a good site for recuperation, but it is not offered as a patriotic symbol of Britain, nor as a permanent location for these friends. Graves, of course, was to leave Britain – as did Richard Aldington and D.H. Lawrence. Sassoon's version of comradeship among soldiers includes the idea of returning home to fight Home, while the French novelist Jules Romains has a vision of bands of comrades marauding as the war breaks down into an anarchy that resembles the Hundred Years' War or the Black Death. And although the idea of a comradeship which may include supersession of family ties is delicately represented in Graves's poem, it remains cognate with the alienations of Remarque's *The Road Back* and of Aldington's fiction, as well as with Lawrence's wanderings and those of Ivor Gurney. If 'Familiar Letter' is linked with 'Two Fusiliers' the valuing of comradeship as a product of war is clear and attractive, but the cost of the product is also recorded, if with typical indirectness.

At times, however, the pressure of the war pushes the idea that experience of it may have value to a poem's margins or beyond. 'Through the Periscope' (a 1915 poem which was published for the first time in *Poems of War*) concerns itself with apathy and death. Its ABAB quatrains are crisp, clear – and awful:

> Trench stinks of shallow buried dead
>   Where Tom stands at the periscope,
> Tired out. After nine months he's shed
>   All fear, all faith, all hate, all hope.

The omission of an article before the poem's first word 'Trench', and the placing of 'Tired out' are the marks of the craftsman; the 'nine months' – perhaps a little obviously – provides a parody of pregnancy; the alliteration of the last line indicates a dreadful levelling diffidence. What follows is neat and seems rather staged – the picture that mixes idyll and ruin; the soldier's thoughts of home, the war and hopelessness – but the last lines parody release from depression:

> But crack!
>   The weary circle's broken
> And a bullet tears through the tired brain.

There is nothing positive about that poem, and if there is in 'The Leveller' it is in the response to 'Old Sergeant Smith, kindest of men'. 'The Leveller' is another quatrain poem (this time AABB) and, again, ostensibly an anecdote. The title is typical of Graves, in that, in alluding to the Levellers of the seventeenth century, it suggests a theme of social equalisation which might have led on to consideration of the war as inducing recognition of man's common humanity. In a sense it does this, but the true levellers are death and, less obviously, the sergeant. The two men 'struck by the same shell' are levelled – 'Together tumbling in one heap' – and the extreme contrast between them rendered nugatory. Actually, the levelling of their difference is more precisely a balance or inversion of the expected. One is 'a pale eighteen-year-old' while the other is a tough exotic who 'came from far-off lands/With bristling chin and whiskered hands' –

> Yet in his death this cut-throat wild
> Groaned 'Mother! Mother!' like a child,

> While that poor innocent in man's clothes
> Died cursing God with brutal oaths.

In response to these deaths, the sergeant copies out 'his accustomed funeral speech/To cheer the womenfolk of each':

> 'He died a hero's death: and we
> His comrades of 'A' Company
> Deeply regret his death: we shall
> All deeply miss so true a pal'.

The fact that this is Sergeant Smith's stock 'speech' obviously indicates another levelling. By implication every member of the company who is killed is a hero and a comrade who will be deeply missed, regardless of the manner of death or the personality of the soldier. But if this subverts commonplace notions of heroism and comradeship, it is only to suggest a deeper truth: the war made all combatants heroes and comrades.

It might be argued that anecdote poems like these are too neat and that Graves's phrasing has, at times, an almost melodramatic quality ('this cut-throat wild/Groaned "Mother! Mother!" like a child'). But they work rather like Sassoon's satirical epigrams, the distancing, sharp outlines and marked contrasts suggestively making a surface simplicity that forces thought. Graves, as a poet of the war, is valuable partly for this reason, that he seems to have thought about it instead of allowing stock response to do his thinking for him.

'A Renascence' – an early poem which Graves wanted, he says, to suppress from *Over the Brazier* – is a good example of how he can modify the commonplace. Very early in the war it became conventional to suggest that it had led to a revival of poetry. This view appears, for instance, in the preface to *Soldier Poets: Songs of the fighting men*, which speaks of 'a new bright efflorescence – a survival and a revival', and which goes on to tell of how the coming of the war 'shocked' the 'braver spirits into poetry and like the larks are heard between the roaring of the guns – the articulated voices of millions of fighting men giving to poetry a new value and significance'.[4] Leaving aside the curious syntax this is a strange statement in some ways. It seems to suggest that verse-writers were braver than those who did not write and (though the phrase is ambiguous) that the 'fighting men' were articulate, as a mass, in verse. But what matters here is the idea of renaissance, one which can be linked both with the concept of the war as cleansing agent and with that of this war as continuous with earlier, 'heroic' history.

Graves's poem ends with a line that agrees with the idea of a renaissance: 'Poetry is born again', the last two words being a translation of 'renascence', which leads back to the title. And the text records a toughening which is also a cleansing:

> White flabbiness goes brown and lean,
> Dumpling arms are now brass bars . . . .

This is better than most versions of the theme because of its particularity, but this account rapidly becomes more complex than at first appears. Arms that become 'brass bars' and the thought that recruits have 'learnt to suffer and live clean' may at first be attractive, because dominated by the opening line's transmutation of 'flabbiness', while the last line of this first quatrain – 'And to think below the stars' – may seem innocent, even banal. At the start of the second stanza 'manliness' is evoked –

> They've steeled a tender, girlish heart,
> Tempered it with a man's pride

– with intimations of knee-jerk sexism and the theme of character beaten out on the anvil of experience. But what has been learnt is 'to play the butcher's part', and at that moment the true significance of 'brass bars', 'steeled' and 'Tempered' emerges, whereby the soldier is less butcher than butcher's tool. All that humanises the instrument is suppressed 'womanliness' ('Though the woman screams inside'), which disturbs the seeming sexism. The 'learning' entails (stanza three) stabbing with 'the stark bayonet' (no swords here) and it culminates in death:

> On Achi Baba's rock their bones
> Whiten, and on Flanders' plain . . . .

'Whiten' and – punningly – 'plain' parody the themes of innocence and cleansing, and it is out of this labour ('their travailings and groans') that 'Poetry is born again'. Graves's poem is a product of this renaissance, an example of what is thought 'below the stars'; and it is a typically poised product, in that the cost of this renaissance is recorded, even while the poem's quality makes the idea of a renaissance valid.

Such redefinition of a commonplace is not entirely negative, for it seeks, while criticising the stock response, to substitute a truer version of the creativity which was a product of the war (rather as

'The Leveller' suggests a democratic redefinition of heroism and comradeship). Elsewhere, Graves characteristically uses history to suggest continuities, to varying effect. 'The Legion' ('Late 1916') is only by implication a poem about the First World War, but the implication is strong enough. It is a dialogue between two professionals. One of these, Strabo, regards the 23rd Legion as dead, 'Dead in the first year of this damned campaign', like the BEF. Survivors, like these two, deserve pity, in Strabo's view, because they've lived 'to see the Legion come to this,/Unsoldierlike, slovenly, bent on loot,/Grumblers, diseased, unskilled to thrust or shoot'. To Gracchus, however, 'The Legion is the Legion'. These 'new men' (slovenly or not) 'all try': Strabo should 'trust their hearts and hands'

> And these same men before the autumn's fall
> Shall bang old Vercingetorix out of Gaul.

Graves's own pride of regiment and the resentful disgust with which veteran soldiers often viewed new recruits are seen here as perennials, but their location in the Gallic wars includes the assurance that the legion/regiment will transmute raw materials. This is reminiscent of those poems of the war which seek to establish heroic continuity,[5] but Graves's account has the detail and toughness to transcend cliché. Another 1916 poem, however, 'Goliath and David', uses history to less positive effect. The bible story of David and Goliath demonstrates that God can help the weak triumph over the strong, and it informs the propaganda of the war, especially around the idea of 'gallant little Belgium' standing up to the German bully. In Graves's poem David has faith ('David, calm and brave,/Holds his ground, for God will save'), but God is not interested ('God's eyes are dim, His ears are shut') and David is killed:

> Steel-helmeted and grey and grim
> Goliath straddles over him.

Here, as elsewhere, Graves keeps an ironic distance – as in the cool 'One cruel backhand sabre-cut', which is almost the voice of the sports correspondent – that works as a way of staying sane, even while it is rewriting comfortable myth-history. The same coolness can work more enigmatically, as in 'The Assault Heroic'. Here fatigue and despair threaten to undermine the psyche –

> We've taken away your hope;

> Now you may droop and mope
> To misery and to death

– but the poet-figure offers defiance of a kind that turns the 'armour' of faith into the defences of the satirist:

> my spear of faith,
> Stout as an oaken rafter,
> With my round shield of laughter,
> With my sharp, tongue-like sword
> That speaks a bitter word,
> I stood beneath the wall
> And there defied them all . . . .

Such defiance is effective –

> My foes were all astounded,
> Dumbstricken and confounded –

and successful:

> I climbed a steep
> Buttress and won the keep,
> And laughed and proudly blew
> My horn . . . .

This chivalric achievement, however, is over inner doubts ('My foes that lay within') and thus belongs to the worlds of *Pilgrim's Progress* and Browning's 'Childe Roland' rather than to that of *El Cid*. And the 'horn' proves to be the call which awakes the dreamer to a new attack by the enemy, evoking memories of the end of Browning's poem or of *The Battle of Maldon*.

'Trench Life' is a sonnet and less coherent than Graves's best work, but it is interesting as offering a variant on the theme of renaissance. Where 'A Renascence' presented poetry reborn from suffering in war, this poem speaks of belief which 'Blossoms from mud', but instead of the cheery banalities of state Anglicanism we have the religion of apocalypse:

> under the rain's whips,
> Flagellant-like we writhe with laughing lips.

This is the world of Norman Cohn's *The Pursuit of the Millennium*,[6] and it has disturbing notes of masochism, writhing applying equally well to pleasure and pain. The point is proleptically made by the text's reference to 'such perverse delight/In utter fear and misery' (ll. 11–12), and the religion is the faith of those driven close to heresy and despair. The revision of official piety is extreme; serene invocations of Christ-with-us on the battlefield are pushed aside as the whips scourge laughing flagellants.

If I understand correctly William Graves's recording of Robert Graves's note on his copy of *Over the Brazier* ('The postcript was added after Loos') the poem 'Big Words' (July 1915) is, in its final form, an interesting example of how Graves can cut away at a comfortingly orthodox stance (although it should be noted that the relationship between the text with and without the postscript is more complicated than it seems without recourse to the note on page 85 of *Poems about War*). The pre-postscript text asserts a readiness to face death. The speaker asserts that, having 'lived those years from roof to cellar-floor', he is 'Ready, as soon as the need comes, to die'. Faith is to be added, for faith has been regained: 'a faith in the wisdom of God's ways . . . finding it justified/Even in this chaos'. So – biblically – 'my cup of praise/Brims over, and I know I'll feel small sorrow . . . If death ends all and I must die to-morrow'. The title – 'Big Words' – is the only thing that ironises this, except perhaps the curious remark (l. 2) about it being 'weak and most ungracious' to whine about death, but the post-Loos postscript wipes out the Brookean posturing:

> But on the firestep, waiting to attack,
> He cursed, prayed, sweated, wished the proud words back.

Perhaps the most devastating of Graves's subversions, however, is the brief couplet poem 'Dead Cow Farm'. This is a creation myth, wherein Adam and Eve are licked into life from 'cold stones and mud' by the 'First Cow', for 'nothing living yet had birth/But elemental Cow on Earth'. The war has brought chaos back, 'Primaeval mud, cold stones and rain', and there is now no cow:

> Here flesh decays and blood drips red,
> And the Cow's dead, the old Cow's dead.

As non-Christian myth this would be disrespectful, but references to Adam and Eve render it (if understandably) blasphemous, suggestive of Ted Hughes's Crow poems.

'To Lucasta . . . ', 'Goliath and David' and 'The Legion' are all examples of poems where Graves looks back in time to use – usually obliquely – aspects of the past with which to compare aspects of the war-present. In the case of 'Goliath and David' the retelling is a reversal of the bible story and, in application to the Great War, includes a reversal of the wished-for outcome. Similar reversals or contrasts are also common at the level of style. So 'When I'm Killed' includes parody-revision of Rupert Brooke:

> When I'm killed, don't think of me
> Buried there in Cambrin Wood . . . .

The parody includes revision of Brooke's rhythm, the adjustment of his syntax towards the colloquial, the substitution of 'When' for 'If', and the giving of a specific location ('Cambrin Wood') for Brooke's vague 'some corner of a foreign field'. A sonnet, 'The Morning before the Battle', utilises the language of Romance but (without really breaking away from that idiom) uses the sestet to achieve a gruesome 'turn'. The octet had presented a melancholy forewarning of death, which 'Blew through the garden' where, walking, the poet-figure had 'Carelessly sang, pinned roses on my breast,/Reached for a cherry-bunch'. Death's coming, in characteristic style, 'blighted every beauty with chill breath' (l. 8). Graves's copy of *Over the Brazier* tells us that he is referring to 'A garden in Béthune near the College des Jeunes Filles', but – in a way which is untypical of Graves – all specificity has been purged, so that the garden is wholly literary. The sestet's turn does not introduce specificity, although its 'violent blows' and 'clotted blood' are unpleasant, while the idea that the now-pale rose 'Smelt sickly' with the vision of the 'wraith' is stock romanticism. More shocking is the conceit of the fruit 'transubstantiate' to 'clotted blood'. This anti-communion replaces salvation with a crop of dead men who 'blossomed in the garden-close'.

Such stylistic contrasts complement the juxtapositions of past and present, making the point that Graves's methods in his poems of the war are frequently binary, as, for example, in 'Sorley's Weather'. In some of his war poems, as already noted, Graves draws on the past to suggest continuities or to establish perspective. Here there is a basic contrast between conditions indoors and out: 'icy rain' and shelter; strong winds and 'firelit study'. The persona is a poet – 'Shall I make a gentle song [?]' – and a lover of the art:

> Tobacco's pleasant, firelight's good:
> Poetry makes both better.

Invoking Romantic poets, he associates them with hedonism:

> Shall I glutton here with Keats?
> Shall I drink with Shelley?

But the final stanza turns away from comfort and such writing:

> Yet rest there, Shelley, on the sill,
>    For though the winds come frorely
> I'm away to the rain-blown hill
>    And the ghost of Sorley.

The poem depends on the Sorley allusion, without which it might seem to involve a rejection of poetry and a perverse embracing of foul weather. Moreover, if the allusion is not understood the poem will hardly be recognised as a war lyric, but the title should immediately alert the informed reader. The reference is to the young Charles Sorley, educated at Marlborough, who enlisted in the Suffolk Regiment in August 1914; served in the trenches as a subaltern; was promoted captain in August 1915; and killed at Loos shortly afterwards. His volume, *Marlborough and other Poems*, was published in 1916 and reached its fifth edition in 1922. Sorley's short life and his verse created a cult almost comparable with Brooke's, but his few poems of the war have (taken together) more complexity than Brooke's and this, in turn, complicates the Graves allusion. If the untitled Sorley poem 'All the hills and vales along' is read as a joyful hymn to nature and death ('Strew your gladness on earth's bed,/So be merry, so be dead'), the Graves reference could be understood to advocate some kind of almost pantheistic stoicism. But Sorley's poem makes better sense as an oblique subversion of jocular stoicism, while another well-known untitled Sorley poem is clearly set against Brooke's sentimentality:

> When you see millions of the mouthless dead
> Across your dreams, in pale battalions go,
> Say not soft things as other men have said,
> That you'll remember . . . .[7]

It is, I think, the sardonic, rather detached element in Sorley which would have attracted Graves, but the main point is that the allusion to Sorley involves a commitment to a contemporary poet as against poets of the past and to a poet of the world beyond that of 'old wine and drowsy meats', this world (via Sorley) being that of the trenches.

If 'Sorley's Weather' uses a past–present contrast, Graves elsewhere has several poems which consider the possibilities of after-war. The early (1915) 'Over the Brazier' presents three visions: the poet-figure's 'cottage in the hills,/North Wales', Willie's dream of Canada, and Mac's 'warm green jewel in the South Sea'. These romanticised locations are, in the final stanza, seen as 'Idyllic dwellings' and the romanticisation is functional, to be set against 'the smoke/And stifling pungency of burning coke'. But it is also a dream which reality has already destroyed for Willie and Mac:

<blockquote>
this silly<br>
Mad War has now wrecked both . . . .
</blockquote>

Therefore

<blockquote>
what<br>
Better hopes has my little cottage got?
</blockquote>

Much later in the war, in 'Peace' ('Summer 1918') Graves returns again to thoughts of his cottage, when, he imagines, in days of peace

<blockquote>
up I climb to twist new thatch<br>
Across my cottage roof . . . .
</blockquote>

But what follows is anxiety about another war:

<blockquote>
shall we seem<br>
To watch a second bristling shadow<br>
Of armed men move across the meadow?
</blockquote>

Graves's poem does, in a sense, register the cliché about 'a war to end wars' ('Will it be over once for all, /With no more killed and no more maimed?'). But there is no strong sense that war has been necessary because of peacetime corruption. Rather, as with Blunden, the feeling seems to be that cessation of blood-letting is a good in itself, whereby peace is largely the condition of not-war. What the poem seeks is non-continuity, without which

<blockquote>
Better we all had died at first,<br>
Better that killed before our prime<br>
We rotted deep in earthy slime.
</blockquote>

That, of course, would be another non-continuity. Here the contrast between war and peace is tenser, more problematic than in 'Over the Brazier'. It is sharper again in 'To R.N.', a 1917 verse-letter to the fellow-poet Robert Nichols. The head-note says that Nichols had told Graves in a letter that he was just finishing his 'Faun' poem: 'I wish you were here to feed him with cherries'. Graves's verse reply is more to do with space than time, except that location and season are coterminous here:

> Cherries are out of season,
> Ice grips at branch and root . . . .

The gap between cherries and ice is, however, also a contrast between verse (or at least the type of verse suggested by the cherries) –

> Drunk with warm melody
> Singing on beds of thyme
> . . . . . . . . . . . .
> Lips dark with juicy stain,
> Ears hung with bobbing fruit

– and the conditions from which the poet-figure writes:

> Here by a snow-bound river
> In scrapen holes . . .
>                  . . . how can I rhyme
> Verses at your desire [?]

The last line has it that 'singing birds are mute'. In context, this means that, as a product of the contrast between war and non-war, Georgian lyricism is dead.

The war and its relationship with after-war continued to trouble Graves after 1918 (which is only to say that he reacted like many other survivors) and the theme is enacted in the long blank verse poem 'A Letter from Wales', which is dated to around 1924, and which begins by focusing on identity:

> This is a question of identity
> Which I can't answer . . . .

The poem is subtitled 'Richard Rolls to his friend, Captain Abel Wright' and is a kind of metaphysical thriller. The identities of both writer and addressee are in doubt:

>                  if you are you
> Who served in the Black Fusiliers with me.
> That is, again, of course, if I am I –

There is evidence that Rolls (the serving fusilier) is dead – as Graves himself was reported dead – and the poet-figure has 'thought lately' that Wright (or his 'representative') 'got killed, /Shot through the throat . . . at Bullecourt' or, alternatively, 'Somewhere in the neighbourhood of Albert,/When you took a rifle bullet through the skull'. Wright is clearly a version of Sassoon. Graves and Sassoon both survived the war; on a literal level Rolls and Wright seem to have done so. But, on another level, that survival is problematic, and the problem, the poem says, has been suppressed by the two men:

> the War
> Was a forbidden ground of conversation.

A revenant ('a relic of the second Richard,/A pack-valise marked with his name and rank') has 'sent me off on a long train of thought': hence the letter and the theory of 'substitution', whereby there were two Rolls and two Wrights. Yet the solution is hardly a solution at all and the poem ends

> 'how am I to put
> The question that I'm asking you to answer?'

If *Goodbye to All That* seeks to exorcise the war, 'A Letter from Wales' suggests that the effort is difficult: the 'substitution view' entails solution through non-continuity.

When, around 1938, Graves wrote his best-known poem of the First World War, it was close to the outbreak of the Second, and this impending war can be seen as validating the doubts of 'Peace'. 'Recalling War' does not seek to say 'goodbye to all that', but it does begin by presenting World War I as assimilated by time and nature:

> Their war was fought these twenty years ago
> And now assumes the nature-look of time . . . .

'Their' – rather than 'My' or 'Our' – is interesting as a way of detachment, but the assurance of this stanza is perhaps deceptive. The flat claims that

> The one-legged man forgets his leg of wood,
> The one-armed man his jointed wooden arm,
> The blinded man sees with his ears and hands
> As much or more than once with both his eyes

remind a reader of disability even as it is disclaimed, and we have already learnt that 'the track aches only when the rain reminds': reduction is not obliteration.

The second stanza asks 'What, then, was war?', and the answer continues the theme of nature, for war was 'an infection of the common sky/That sagged ominously'. The response to its oppression was the thrusting out of 'Boastful tongue, clenched fist and valiant yard' – the response of patriotism and chivalry. This, in stanza three, is extended and qualified. Fear produced a sickness of delight that issued in an emphasis upon body at the expense of thought:

> Never was such antiqueness of romance,
> Such tasty honey oozing from the heart.

War also produced awareness of 'old importances' that even included God – as 'A word of rage in lack of meat, wine, fire,/In ache of wounds.' But war was also – and the sequence says definitively – that which displaced all this:

> War was return of earth to ugly earth,
> War was foundering of sublimities,
> Extinction of each happy art and faith . . . .

From such extinction, at the striking of the 'unendurable moment', all that there is is 'The inward scream, the duty to run mad'. And so, finally, the retrospection rewrites the poem's opening with a necessary defensive facetiousness:

> And we recall the merry ways of guns –
> Nibbling the walls of factory and church
> Like a child, piecrust

– and this sight is 'to be recalled in elder days' as

> learnedly the future we devot
> To yet more boastful visions of despair.

This recalling says (with the picking up of 'boastful' from the second stanza) that the poem's knowledge of the war in retrospect leads nowhere: if war is 'natural' it is in a grimly cyclic sense. But the effort at detachment in 'Their war' has also failed: '*we* devote'.

The poems Graves wrote about the war range across more than twenty years. He adopts a variety of approaches, verse forms and linguistic registers, making use of history, contrasts, reportage, satire, Romanticism, Georgianism . . . to represent his sense of war experience. Yet there is a consistent effort at distance and detachment, a coolness and a wearing of masks, that is continuous with the fictionalised autobiography of *Goodbye to All That*. To tell the truth, Graves becomes a fabulator, this being a way of coping or of evading the 'duty to run mad'. Thomas Kyd's Hieronimo, in *The Spanish Tragedy*, had run mad, and bitten out his tongue to evade speech. Graves becomes polyglot and stayed sane. In the language of 'A Letter from Wales' he does this through the device of 'representatives': 'My substitution view'. So sanity, under war's pressure, entails the division of personality: a damaged sanity at best. The attempts at distance also suggest a distaste for war (a distaste which is wholly sane) and almost the desire not to write about it. Graves's efforts to suppress his recordings of the war represent a denial that he has written about it. Paradoxically, the quality of the best of his poems about the war makes it appropriate that he failed to suppress them.

## Notes

1. Robert Graves, *Poems About War,* ed. William Graves, Cassell, 1988, p. 7.
2. ibid.
3. All references to Robert Graves's poems are to William Graves's edition (note 1, above).
4. Erskine MacDonald, 1916, p. 9.
5. See p. 103f.
6. Secker and Warburg, 1957.
7. *The Poems and Selected Letters,* ed. H.D. Spear, Blackness Press, 1978.

# 8

# RECEPTION AND VALUING

You begin with a body of work and you finish with a selection. Any critical work, any anthology, is a story with this plot, its structures being an account of how the writer or anthologist gets from 'body of work' to 'selection'. There are, of course, cases where the 'body of work' is quite sharply defined: the number of surviving Elizabethan sonnets or the total output of Samuel Richardson are knowable within limits. 'The Poetry of the First World War' is, however, far more problematic. Does 'Poetry' include all verse? Is 'best' to be assumed between 'The' and 'Poetry'? Does 'of' mean 'issuing from the period of', or 'about', or both simultaneously? What, if 'of' means 'about', is to be included?

Writers and anthologists who have concerned themselves with verse that is in some way related to the First World War have tended (consciously or not) to mediate between the terms 'Poetry' and 'First World War', and the selections they have made necessarily represent the results of this mediation. If the emphasis is on 'Poetry' in essentialist or idealist terms the raw material of the verse of the war will be sifted with reference to what the critic or anthologist understands to be permanent standards and/or absolute criteria. A purely aesthetic application of such an approach (if such is possible) would, finally, see the war, as represented in its verse, as no more than a body of material from which Great Art might come. If, however, the First World War is regarded as, historically, the most important event of our century, and if the relevant verse is seen as part of the recording of that event and its repercussions, it might follow that the very fact of recording should dominate over ideas of absolute standards of literary excellence. Beyond this, an historicist approach could be to argue that noticing, say, 'inflated rhetoric' in the verse of Rupert Brooke – defining this in terms of some absolute criterion of proper diction for verse – is only the beginning of an enquiry which should go on to consider what socio-cultural conditions produced this inflation and what the latter signifies about the former. In such a case, it is the 'deficiency' which is the instructive, illuminating factor.

Both terms mentioned above – 'Poetry' and 'The First World War' – are, however, less sharp-edged than they may seem. A belief in an absolute called 'Poetry' needs to take account of a historical record which suggests that such a belief is either subjective, or chimerical, or platonic; a problem that is evaded rather than solved by phrases like 'changing tastes in poetry'. The latter would be charted, so far as the poetry of the First World War is concerned, by the comparative examination of the critical reception of, say, Brooke, Robert Nichols and Isaac Rosenberg, to the conclusion, perhaps, that the passage of several decades has seen 'changes of taste', as a result of which Rosenberg is superior to Brooke and Nichols. This leaves the possibility of further changes and associated revaluations; and an absolutist would need to argue that one taste or other reflects Poetry as an absolute excellence. The First World War itself may be seen as a self-evident fact, but it is only so as a tolerated generalisation, since most of what defines it, beyond a few generally accepted dates, is unstable. The valuing of the concept 'war' is itself unfixed. Since for me 'war' is always a disaster and almost always unjustifiable, I am open to the charge of undervaluing qualities displayed in war (and, of course, to the cruder charges of being a coward or idealist). There is basic disagreement among people about how far war is inevitable in the conduct of human affairs, as about the qualities (and valuation of qualities) which war generally or any particular war could be said to instil into participants. More specifically, there is disagreement about the policy of attrition in the First World War, about the contribution of the tank and gas, about the treatment of deserters and the value or otherwise of Douglas Haig, about the sinking of the 'Lusitania' and the execution of Edith Cavell. Neither the causes nor the effects of the war are agreed on, while what exactly the war meant for different people is very various and often unknowable.

It is, therefore, not surprising that the history of the reception of poetry of the war is one which involves consideration both of material factors and vicissitudes of valuing, the two being at times interrelated. An anthologist from the period of the First World War like E.B. Osborn, concerned to promote a positive version of poetry in the war effort, may well have been unsympathetic to the attitudes developed by such a poet as Wilfred Owen, but Owen's poetry was not readily available to Osborn. Moreover, if the poetry of the war is represented only by poetry written during its formal timespan, much of the best of Ivor Gurney must be excluded, as well as important poems by such as Blunden, Graves and Sassoon. In the case of Gurney, other material factors kept his work marginalised until quite recently – problems of textual access and authority, issues of the definition of madness. And it has taken the revival of feminism to promote even a degree of recognition for the poetry of war written by women.

Such factors suggest some of the ways in which obvious material conditions have influenced the valuing of poetry of the war, and it is easy enough to establish that both general interest in such poetry and in individual poets has changed since the war came to an end. An analysis of items in the *Annual Bibliography*, for instance, indicates a striking increase in critical attention to poetry of the war since 1960.[1] It also shows that up to that time Rupert Brooke was the poet who received most critical and scholarly attention, but that from 1945 Wilfred Owen begins to rival Brooke and, since 1960, has been overwhelmingly the First World War poet most often attended to. Edmund Blunden seems to have had a modest stable standing since 1920, while Rosenberg and Gurney are largely products of the last two decades. The overhauling of Brooke by Owen can, obviously enough, be seen in terms of a shift in taste – from war as heroic to 'tragic waste' – but relating this shift to its chronology of reception is complicated. It looks as if it may have taken the Second World War to effect a critico-scholarly displacement which had taken place, in verse itself, within the timespan of the First.

Quite marked variations of valuing are also evident in modern anthologies of poetry of the war. The six anthologies of the past twenty-five years which I have analysed are consistent in the prominence with which Owen and Sassoon are featured, but other figures receive various treatment. Thus, Rosenberg is second only to Owen in Jon Silkin's anthology, but is represented by a mere four poems in Hussey's. Hussey prints more poems by Gurney than by any other poet, but Gurney is completely excluded by Gardner, Parsons and Black. Uncertainties about what constitutes war poetry are exemplified in the case of Edward Thomas: Gardner and Black omit Thomas; Hibberd/Onions print three poems (the same number as for Harold Begbie and Frederic Manning); Silkin includes twelve (the same as the ration for Blunden, and fewer only than for Owen and Rosenberg). Another change is evident if the poets most fully represented by Osborn during the war are sought in these post-1960 collections. Most have vanished. Osborn printed eleven poems by Robert Nichols, who still finds a place in modern anthologies, but a much reduced one. F.W. Harvey (six poems in Osborn) is scarcely visible now, while Willoughby Weaving (also six poems in Osborn) survives in the single poem printed by Gardner. The representation of women has been commented on earlier.[2]

What matters is not the fact that representation in anthologies or citation in critical writing varies in this way, but what such facts signify. It is obvious enough to anyone who reads poetry of the war at all widely that the war, as represented in verse, looks importantly different if Gurney is omitted from an anthology purporting to represent the war in some way. If an editor decides that Edward Thomas is not a poet of the war, any reader of such an editor's anthology will be deprived of an important aspect of how the war was registered while it was going on. Similar limitations happen if women poets are omitted or if an anthology is confined to combatants. Again, overtones of valuing and selections from a notional full picture are indicated by the number of poets who are included in an anthology: Silkin has 22 'English' poets, Gardner 68, Hibberd/Onions 114. The number of poets may be affected by such considerations as the contractual length of the volume, but the important point remains that decisions of this kind affect how such versions of poetry of the war are constructed and thus how the war itself is seen.

An extreme example of how selection means distortion is St John Adcock's memorial volume *For Remembrance*. This incorporates twenty-six portraits. All but three are of subalterns. Of the others, Francis Ledwidge ('Lance-Corporal') was a known Georgian before the war; Leslie Coulson ('Sergt') was a journalist; and Alexander Robertson ('Corporal') seems to have been to Oxford. No ranker is portrayed. The portraits are not all stylised to a single stereotype, but nothing like the war portraits of Gurney, Rosenberg or T.B. Clark appears. As Adcock presents it, the war is an affair of young patrician subalterns who do not love war, but who – understanding its necessity – give their lives joyously. There is no need to be cynical about Adcock's volume, but it is very evidently an interpretation of the war. In the same way (but to quite different effect) the sections into which Black's 1979 anthology is divided construct an interpretation: Early Visions, Puzzled Questioning, Realism on the Western Front, The Pity of It, Bitter Satire. In fact, this suggests a double interpretation – that of the editor and that of the poets themselves – and one that moves progressively from vision, through realism, to satire. Black's organisation and selection can be defended, albeit at some cost to chronology (remembering, in particular, how much pro-war verse was written late in the war), but it offers a rather different view to that created by E.B. Osborn, whose sections include The Mother Land, The Christian Soldier, School and College, Chivalry of Sport and Loving and Living.

## RECEPTION AND SOME ANTHOLOGIES

Volumes which represent the responses of various individuals to the First World War while it was still going on began to appear soon after the fighting started; and they offer, in their organisation and selection of poems, accounts of the war itself. I shall concentrate here on two anthologies: *More Songs by the Fighting Men* and *The Muse in Arms*.

*More Songs . . .* was published in December 1917, by which time much of the war's more awful fighting had taken place, and was a sequel to *Soldier Poets*. It cost 2/6 in cloth and there was a 'trench' edition at 1/6. The cover of my copy claims that the volume provides 'A representative collection of new poems' and the poets included are then listed: forty-two of them. So far as this volume is concerned, war poetry is verse by combatants. None of the now best known names appears and, in effect, the poetry of the war is officer-poetry. Only four of the writers are described as privates, while sixteen are non-commissioned officers and the rest commissioned. This, as with every anthology I know of, represents an obvious imbalance, not necessarily of the amount of verse written within the relevant categories, but certainly with reference to the officer: men ratio. Of the twenty-six commissioned officers, eighteen are lieutenants. This version of the war is that of very young junior officers at the Front, close to the stereotype outlined in Chapter 1. Although none of the most famous names appears, there are several which can be found in modern anthologies – Leslie Coulson, Paul Bewsher,

P.H.B. Lyon.

The short publisher's note which occurs on the inside flyleaf, after extracts from reviews of *Soldier Poets,* suggests that 'The national spirit would be fortified if every adult and every adolescent were acquainted with' that volume; and the impulse behind *More Songs* is the same. In his brief preface Galloway Kyle (writing as of *The Poetry Review,* but also managing director of the volume's publisher, Erskine MacDonald) directs a reader's expectations. The poetry is 'typical of the lyrical efflorescence of the fighting men'. It is to be seen as 'more severe' (i.e. more experienced) than the 'songs before sunrise' of *Soldier Poets,* but it shows 'spiritual quickening' (with intimations of cleansing) and shares with the earlier volume 'the high clean spirit of ardent, generous youth engaged on a new Crusade'. Kyle associates his poets with the Elizabethans, 'with whom, in the great comradeship beyond the grave', they march to 'continue the material and spiritual warfare', directing the fight that will not end with the war'. Kyle's running metaphor is of pregnancy, labour and birth. The war is a pregnancy and there are hints of a Messiah. What is perhaps most important is that the war is seen as a positive, in having given rise to a new, pure lyricism which transcends the weariness of pre-war and the distresses of combat experience. These poets, we are to understand, 'are nobly free from that realism which thinks a stench more real than a perfume'. 1917 was not a good year for the Allies, but Kyle's account suggests unshaken confidence. The poems are arranged alphabetically by author, but the volume is none the less shaped by its editor's view of the war. So it opens with sapper Eric de Banzie's sonnet 'The Gift', which speaks of the war as 'a grand boon' granted by God and ends with the patriotic 'so England lives!', and concludes with Lieutenant Walter Wilkinson's 'Night in War Time' (also, significantly, a sonnet), which finishes:

> Yet slowly, surely darkness dies: and then,
> Out of the deep night's menace, dawns the day!

The war is seen as having been a reawakening, but both Kyle's birth metaphor and Wilkinson's dawning suggest that the full consequences will only emerge when the war has been won. It is this that makes the experience worthwhile; and *More Songs* offers a poetry of the First World War that largely denies the possibility of a negative reading, while also suggesting that all ranks are united, feeling the 'national spirit'.

My text of *The Muse in Arms* is more pretentious, in hard covers and with a gold emblem on the front which combines the lyre, the sword and laurels in an anachronistic but potent image. The anthology was first published in November 1917, 'edited, with an introduction, by E.B. Osborn'. It purports to be mainly a collection of poems 'written in the field of action', and it is a very carefully arranged volume.

Osborn provides quite an elaborate introduction, and he is frank about the anthology's purpose – 'to show what passes in the British warrior's soul when . . . he has glimpses of the ultimate significance of warfare' (p. v). The selection ('which can claim to be fairly representative') shows the warrior's capacity 'for remembering the splendour and forgetting the squalor' (cf. Kyle on realism, above), and the 'sunny joyousness' of men who 'gloried in the thought of the great ordeal' (p. vi). To the British, war is properly a sport and linked to chivalry (p. vii). British warriors do not show hatred (pp. xiii–xiv) and Germany will necessarily fail because of having too much science and too little poetry (p. xv). But it turns out that British poetry of the war is especially the product of 'famous schools and ancient universities', and one of its strengths is conservatism ('For the most part . . . conventional forms . . . and . . . the conventional currency of thought'). The spirit of these warrior-poets is what will permit hope in 'the hard days of the coming peace-time' (p. xxi). Osborn stresses a continuity with the past that is anachronistic: a conventional output of ancient universities is the ultimate weapon, and so the traditional lyre is stronger than modern technology.

There are poems by fifty-two writers in *The Muse in Arms*. Only two are women (Roma White and Dorothy Plowman), while five are identified by initials or pseudonyms. Of the forty-five remaining, thirty-eight are officers, mainly captains and lieutenants, the proportion of officers being higher even than in *More Songs* . . . . Like Kyle's, Osborn's war is that of young officers serving at the Front: his List of Authors, which precedes the main body of text, provides basic information on rank, and marks those contributors known to have been killed (thus poignantly emphasising those sacrificed in 'the great ordeal'). By comparison with Kyle's volume, Osborn's does contain poems by poets now considered as among the most significant voices from the war. Owen, Rosenberg, Thomas and Blunden are all absent, but there are two poems by Sassoon, four by Gurney and three by Graves. Against this, however, there are, as we have seen, six by Harvey, six by Weaving, and eleven by Nichols. The poems are organised into sections (as also noted above) which offer positive, hopeful versions of the nature and purpose of the war. Osborn's claim of fair representation is faintly supported by the token inclusion of two women and by the presence of poems (like Graves's 'Big Words' and Sassoon's 'The Rear-Guard') which are sardonic rather than elevated. Yet the anthology remains true to its introduction. The female representation is perfunctory. Roma White's 'News of Jutland' may have been included because of the paucity of naval poems of the war, while Dorothy Plowman's 'Any Soldier's Wife' simply reinforces ideas of unity and support, symbolising the alleged oneness of Front and Home. And although Osborn does include some sardonic writing, it is relatively rare and contained within the prevailingly positive assertions of the collection. It can, though, at least be said that a reading of *The Muse in Arms* indicates that a few did not go cheerfully to their fates.

Robert Nichols's *Anthology of War Poetry 1914–1918* was published in the latter part of the Second World War (1943).[3] It can be seen as bridging the period between the anthologies of the First World War itself and those of post-1960. Its date is interesting not only because it places the anthology of poems of one war in the context of another, but because it can be seen as a late example of that revival of interest in the 1914–18 war which produced, among others, Remarque's *All Quiet on the Western Front* (1929), Manning's novel *Her Privates We* (1930), Sassoon's *Memoirs of an Infantry Officer* (1930) and his *Sherston's Progress* (1936), David Jones's *In Parenthesis* (1937) and Wyndham Lewis's *Blasting and Bombardiering* (1937). There is also the fact that Nichols had been, if briefly, a combatant in the First World War, his anthology being a retrospect, in the same way (though in a different form) as Manning's novel and Sassoon's memoirs.

The table of contents contains only fourteen named poets and the dominant representatives approximate to those of more modern anthologies. Although Rosenberg, Thomas and Gurney are all ignored, Sassoon (thirteen poems), Blunden (nine) and Graves (eight) are strongly present. Brooke is represented by five sonnets and Owen by four poems (as many as Francis Brett Young). It is thus possible to sense a weakening of Brooke's position, while the relatively slight presence of Owen is partly offset by the warm praise of his work in the preface. This preface is preceded by a dedication that consists of Scott-Moncrieff's translation of the last lines of the *Chanson de Roland*, together with G.K. Chesterton's remarks on those lines. Chesterton says that the *Chanson* ends 'as it were, with a vision and vista of war against the barbarians; and the vision is true. For that war is never ended, which defends the sanity of the world against all the stark anarchies and rending negations which war against it for ever.' He also comments on 'That high note of a forlorn hope, of a host at bay and a battle against odds without end'. Given that this anthology appeared in 1943, the dedication links the two world wars with each other and as part of an unending struggle. There are suggestions of chivalric war, but instead of the cavalier note there is that of the forlorn hope, as in the *Chanson* and 'The Battle of Maldon' – and, of course, the war on the Western Front was not going well for the Allies in 1943.

The preface – a dialogue between the anthologist and Julian Trevelyan, who represents the interlocutor of a younger generation – is longer than the text. It stresses that 'poetic merit' is the 'sole criterion of choice', as against 'propaganda either for or against war as an instrument of policy', this policy being adopted in the hope of finding readers, 'more particularly, I hoped, among your generation' (p. 18). This claim cannot but be disingenuous, and the specific comments on individual poets and aspects of the First World War have no choice but to subvert the ostensibly 'pure' intention. The sense of speaking particularly to a younger generation which has limited knowledge of the First World War is strong, in the provision of information about, for example, Sorley and in the confident, donnish judgements: 'I consider the poems of Wilfred Owen by far the most beautiful written during the war' (p. 96); The Poet Laureate 'once said to me . . . that, had Sorley lived, he might have become our greatest dramatist since Shakespeare' (p. 36). Both preface and text suggest a loss of innocence. The inadequacy of chivalry in face of 'the scientific method' (compare Osborn) and 'the brutal literalness' of 'modern weapons of precision' are noted (p. 80), while the dominant tones of the text are those of Sassoon, Blunden and Graves. The last words of the text proper are Owen's – 'weep, you may weep, for you may touch them not' ('Greater Love'). The king of the *Chanson* was, in the dedication, also weeping:

Tears filled his eyes, he tore his snowy beard.

Nichols's anthology is one of endurance.

This anthology appeared while the Second World War was still going on, while editors of more modern anthologies of the First World War have worked in a period deeply marked by the experiences of 1939–45. How this might affect a view of 1914–18 is not difficult to see. The idea of the First World War being a war to end war makes little or no sense given a second global conflict, for example, while the challenge of Nazism put pacifist views under great pressure; against which atoms bombs dropped on Hiroshima and Nagasaki were a new and awful demonstration of war's destructiveness.

Jon Silkin's *Penguin Book of First World War Poetry* (1979) has probably been the most influential anthology of the post-1945 period. Silkin is himself a poet; he had written a book-length study of First World War poetry[4] before editing the Penguin collection; while *Stand*, of which he was and is co-editor, has shown interest in poetry of the First World War while being one of the more internationally-minded of British literary periodicals.

Silkin contributed a sixty-two-page introduction. This, as with Nichols, means that the poems which make up the main text are approached by a serial reader in the light of an elaborate and even aggressive contextualisation. Moreover, Silkin's anthology strikes against the insularity of other such collections. He was not the first to include poems from North America, but he devotes the last part of his text to translations from such continental poets as Trakl and Ungaretti, thus reminding readers that the English response to the war should properly be seen as part of a much wider phenomenon. This desire to widen the context for English poetry of the war (which, among other things, makes the point that the English poetry is more conservative than the German) is also evident in Silkin's introduction. Silkin's first words, for instance, make it clear that his is to be a 'committed' volume: 'Even compassion must now be circumspect, for if it doesn't try to do away with, or limit, that war that causes the suffering, it's indulgent.' When later (p. 29) we read of 'the fourth and last stage of compassion, where the anger and compassion are merged, with extreme intelligence, into an active desire for change, a change that will re-align the elements of human society in such a way as to make it more creative and fruitful', we should be fully aware that Silkin is not seeking to construct a dispassionate historical or critical account of the war or its poetry. There is a literary-historical dimension, mainly that of English

Romanticism, but it is defined in terms of 'a consciously political ethos' (p. 12). Silkin's Romantics anticipate 'the positions of the First World War Poets' (p. 25) – but not primarily for reasons of style (aesthetically speaking).

The association of anger, compassion, extreme intelligence and an active desire for change goes a long way to defining excellence for Silkin, who is explicit that the latter is his concern ('I was in the end concerned with excellence' – p. 70 – and 'no anthology as far as I know has tried to limit itself to excellence' – p. 72). But it is important to stress that, for Silkin, excellence is not primarily an aesthetic matter. The quality of response dictates the representation of different poets – 'the reader will be correct in thinking that the more poems there are by a poet the more highly I think of him' (p. 70) – but the quality has been carefully defined in the context of the revolutionary aspect of Romanticism. In this sense Silkin's anthology seeks to place the best poetry of the First World War in the context of revolutionary struggle to ameliorate the human condition. So seen, excellence produces emphasis on Owen, Rosenberg, Sassoon, Blunden and Thomas. Silkin prints more poems (eighteen) by Owen than any other modern editor I have looked at, and substantially more Rosenberg (seventeen), Thomas (twelve) and Blunden (twelve). This means a marked distortion of the record, but only if we are looking for an anthology of 'typical' responses. To be of 'extreme intelligence' and to have both anger and compassion is, in Silkin's terms, not to be typical. When Silkin prints seventeen poems by Rosenberg, as against Parsons' eight or Gardner's four, he is making a statement about Rosenberg's significance in a context in which creative gifts are to be seen as properly serving 'an active desire for change'. So Silkin is at an opposite pole to Osborn, who sees conservatism as the great feature of the war's poetry.

Silkin's Penguin anthology is challenged (more implicitly than explicitly) by Dominic Hibberd and John Onions, in their *Poetry of the Great War* (1986). This is the most serious critical anthology of English poetry of the war to have been published, in the sense that it comments extensively on earlier collections and criticism, seeks to provide a full apparatus of notes and is strenuously committed to the importance of dating. The emphasis is on materiality (what can be said about the particular circumstances under which specific work was produced) and the editors oppose 'assumed progression from idealism to bitterness' (p. 4). So, although 'We have arranged the book by theme', 'The parts are not intended as a rigid framework' (p. 7). The awareness of the complexity of the situation is salutary: 'there was a continuous development throughout the war, though the work of individuals developed at different times and in different ways or in some cases scarcely changed at all' (p. 14). Throughout a substantial introduction there are corrections of misrepresentations, and the anthology provides the fullest handbook we have. Although the rough guide provided by the number of poems per poet is orthodox (in modern terms) – Sassoon (fourteen), Owen (eleven), Gurney (eight), Rosenberg and Graves (seven), Blunden (six) – Hibberd and Onions include far more poets than Silkin did, offering a much wider spectrum of response and being more concerned to locate poems in material conditions.

In passing, Hibberd and Onions remark that 'Silkin's case is a personal one, based on – and appealing to – a radical political commitment' (p. 4). Their own anthology purports, it would seem, to be neutral. It is not concerned with 'excellence' and (despite the deployment of Gurney as postcript) does not go much beyond a liberal humanist sense that war is unpleasant. To an extent the editors seem to see their work as archaeological: '[The verse] remains as a unique and still largely unresearched chapter in British social and literary history' (p. 32). Taken together, the Silkin and Hibberd/ Onions anthologies show versions of a challenge to issues of valuing: how do we/how should we value the English verse product of the First World War?


VALUING


To ask the question in this form is perhaps absurd, since, once we reflect for a moment, it seems obvious that there are many reason-able answers, which amounts to saying that how we value this material depends on where we are coming from; what context there is for the question. Thus, it would seem that, for Michael Hamburger, the answer is 'hardly at all'. In his *The Truth of Poetry: Tensions in modern poetry from Baudelaire to the 1960s* he has a chapter called 'Internationalism and war',[5] but Hamburger's contin-ental and American dimensions mean that English poets of the First World War are of marginal interest (which, in part, makes a point about how shallow the hold of Modernism was on English culture of the early twentieth century). For Boris Ford, editing volume seven of *The Pelican Guide to English Literature*,[6] the literary product of the war demands attention. The result, however, is a short essay by D.J. Enright called 'The literature of the First World War' which at once elides 'literature' into 'poetry' (an interesting valuation in itself) and rapidly reduces 'poetry of the First World War' to the work of Owen, Sassoon and – more briefly – Rosenberg. But Enright does, in passing, pause to ask of Sassoon's 'Suicide in the trenches', 'Not poetry, perhaps? But does this matter?' (p. 159) – a question to which we shall return. His essay uneasily evades the contrasts between Silkin and Hibberd/Onions. John Lucas, writing *Modern English Poetry – from Hardy to Hughes*, is concerned with ideas and traditions of Englishness and these define the context within which he considers the poetry of the Great War.[7] In such an account of English poetry over about a century, the war's verse demands a chapter, its value, however, being what it suggests about Englishness, Lucas rightly noticing that the war could hardly fail to raise questions about such concepts.

You get different answers, then, depending on the framework within which the question is asked. If 'modern poetry' is defined internationally, English poetry of the war has little weight; if you are concerned with modern English poetry at the level of stylistic innovation you may not get much beyond Owen's pararhyme, although if the approach is broader – concentrating upon how native traditions interact with Continental and/or American ones – Thomas and Gurney should demand attention. If you start from the view that the First World War was a major twentieth-century phenomenon it is possible either to see its poetry as of no interest to the historian[8] or to consider it as a 'unique chapter in English social and literary history' (Hibberd/Onions, above). Another version of this might be to ponder the gap between the significance of the war and the mediocrity of much of its literature – a gap which suggests major issues about life, literature and culture at large. Noting the technical conservatism which seems to have pleased Osborn, and which is matched by a conservatism of attitude, raises important questions about British insularity and about the nature and value of tradition. And so you might return to the anthologies of Silkin and Hibberd/Onions, seeing in them paradigmatic statements of irreconcilable positions: the war's poetry is either valued for a particular kind of excellence, manifest in a very small proportion of the total product, or for reasons which are socio-archaeological. If, not far behind Silkin's position, there is the figure of F.R. Leavis (but with a greater political radicalism than anything Leavis ever showed), there is, lurking behind Hibberd/Onions, something like modern 'new historicism', with its associated awareness of post-structuralism and modern linguistics.

Dominic Hibberd's 1981 selection of critical comments on First World War poetry provides a convenient text for discussion of the critical reception of the poetry.[9] Obviously, such a selection, going back as far as 1914, can only choose among what material is available, and – equally – will reflect the interests of the selector. Hibberd opens his introduction by remarking that 'There were thousands, probably millions, of poems written in English during the First World War; critical opinion has never taken more than a very small number of them into account.' He then points out that, in each of three chronological sections of his collection, a general subsection is followed by 'studies of individual poets'. Nine poets in all are represented in this way: 'The nine are not selected according to any theoretical definition of the category "war poet", they are simply those authors whose poetry about the war seems to have attracted most critical attention.' Perhaps inevitably, Hibberd thus helps perpetuate a hierarchy which the anthology he later produced with John Onions suggests he is opposed to. But the outcome is revealing. The index helps here, indicating that criticism has interested itself most in Owen (above all), Rosenberg and Sassoon, with Blunden, Brooke, Graves, Yeats and Hardy making up the second division: Gurney (one reference) is the most strikingly neglected figure; while the ignoring of poetry by women suggests (among other things) that criticism has concentrated heavily on verse written by combatants. All of the nine poets who receive individual attention were combatants, as are all those most prominent in the index, with the exceptions of Yeats and Hardy, whose presence has more to do with their importance in twentieth-century English poetry than with their contributions to poetry of the war. The neglect of Gurney means that Rosenberg is the only voice from the ranks.

Such emphasis and omissions reflect quite accurately the history of the reception of poetry of the First World War. Apart from the enthusiasm of such as Kyle and Osborn for the 'songs' of the now largely-unknown poets they anthologise, there has been very little serious criticism of the poems written outside the circle of the 'best'. This circle has largely been deemed to exclude male non-combatants, while women's poetry of the war received virtually no attention until Reilly's anthology and Khan's critical study. It took Kavanagh's edition to get Gurney established outside a narrow band of enthusiasts, while there has been little attention paid to the matter of voices from the ranks. Poetry of the First World War is understood, in the critical story, to be the verse of young men serving as subalterns on the Western Front.

All this having been said, it may be revealing to look at how three key figures have been received, as this reception is recorded by Hibberd, before considering more general aspects of the critical response.

The first of my three, Rupert Brooke, can be dealt with quite briefly, the reception of his work being inextricably bound up with the Brooke legend and exemplifying rather neatly how reaction is connected with the recipient's questions. Winston Churchill's remarks in *The Times* obituary of April 1915 constitute a public response which actively helps to construct the legend and which presents Brooke as a public representative figure having 'A voice . . . to do justice to the nobility of our youth in arms'. The 'thoughts to which he gave expression . . . will be shared by many thousands of young men moving resolutely and blithely forward' in the war. This 'poet-soldier' had 'the simple force of genius'. Brooke is the bard of the young male soldiers; he is neither individual nor complex. Genius is 'simple' and speaks for others. But, at almost the same moment, a private response by another 'poet-soldier' said different things. To Charles Sorley, in a letter of 28 April 1915, Brooke's war sonnets were selfish poems:

> He is far too obsessed with his own sacrifice, regarding the going to war of himself (and others) as a highly intense, remarkable and sacrificial exploit, whereas it is merely the conduct demanded of him (and others) by the turn of circumstances, where non-compliance with this demand would have made life intolerable . . . . He has clothed his attitude in fine words; but he has taken the sentimental attitude.

But this sharp comment could be rewritten: Brooke's obsession may well have been egotistic, but, representing a glamorous egotism, it had considerable propaganda value. Churchill and Sorley notice similar features, but respond differently.

By the time Donald Davie touched on Brooke in his *New*

*Statesman* article of 1964, Brooke was no longer *the* poet of the First World War, and Davie depicts a Brooke along lines that echo Churchill only to subvert him. Davie speaks of Brooke as a 'professional', over against the 'amateurs', Grenfell and Sorley; and this has a useful double reference. It reminds us that Brooke was an experienced and quite versatile poet before the war began, but also that his war sonnets were, in effect, both offered and received as public verse, serving what was seen as the nation's need. But Davie then defines this professionalism in deadly fashion: 'Brooke . . . has to be, in every corrupted sauvity of style . . . the professional master of language, the expensively schooled rhetorican.' For Davie, Brooke is not 'a bad, a hollow and dishonest and heartless poet', but 'the English soldier of 1914'. If seen as such, Brooke should continue to be of significance, even though Davie's labelling of Brooke needs careful scrutiny.

Siegfried Sassoon attracted interesting comment as early as the second half of the war itself, part of this interest inhering in how critics dealt with the aesthetic and moral issues his verse raised. H.W. Massingham sees Sassoon as the poet of 'truth about the actual conditions of the war' and is aware of 'the deadly criticism' that lies beneath the poems. Sassoon's poems are 'modern epigrams': 'they have nothing to do with poetry', but 'to our mind, Mr Sassoon is quite right to select this method' (epigrams) 'to discharge the hot fluid of his scorn'. For Massingham, it seems, 'poetry' must be something other than what Sassoon devotes himself to, with the implication that the war has rendered poetry irrelevant. In place of ideas of craft we have the image of 'hot fluid' (blood? semen?). For Edmund Gosse (also in 1917) the possible danger which Sassoon represents to national morale is disturbing. Sassoon is no true cynic: his 'is the rage of disenchantment, the violence of a young man . . . who, finding the age out of joint, resents being called upon to help to mend it'. Sassoon's sentiments 'must tend to relax the effort of the struggle', but Gosse recognises that these sentiments have been 'conducted with so much honesty and courage'. Sassoon is Hamlet, honourable but dangerous. Virginia Woolf, however, comes closer to Massingham. Sassoon is a teller of truths about the war, and Woolf avoids the 'poetry or not' issue by transcending it ('as if it were a matter of indifference to him whether you called him poet or not') and by suggesting that, somehow, there is 'a stage of suffering' such that 'beauty and art have something too universal about them' to be of use. If, for Woolf, Sassoon is not a poet, it is not because of ineptitude (he is 'so evidently able-bodied in his poetic capacity') but because his material defies/denies the category.

In the same year (1918) Middleton Murry saw Sassoon's verse in similar terms, but he is clear that Sassoon is not a poet. Rather, he is a versifier of incoherent cries. Reading Sassoon's verse 'we feel, not as we do with true art, which is the evidence of a man's triumph over his experience, that something has, after all been saved from disaster, but that everything is irremediably and intolerably wrong'. Murry agrees that 'something is wrong': 'Why should one of the finest creatures of the earth be made to suffer a pain so brutal that he can give it no expression, that even this most human and mighty relief is denied him?' Murry goes on to describe aspects of Sassoon's verse quite accurately, and to elucidate his own view of art, but what matters is already evident. If Murry's response is accurate, he has either marked the point at which art fails human experience, or Sassoon's poetry and the circumstances which produced it call for a new definition of art, or a new art.

Sassoon's achievement has continued to elicit various, sometimes troubled responses. Edmund Blunden – a fellow 'poet-soldier' looking back from 1939 – stresses Sassoon's 'poetic nature trained in patient watchings for the significant thing and the correspondingly significant phrase', and the dedication of this poetic nature to achieving 'a complete impression, such as must command the attention and understanding even of the unitiated' of 'the whirlpool of danger, and labour, and noise' of the war. Jon Silkin's comments implicitly accept that Sassoon has 'poetic capacity', while Bernard Bergonzi stresses 'the inherent limits of Sassoon's . . . satirical approach'; 'Sassoon remains fundamentally a poet of narrow but direct effects'.

The chief features of Sassoon's main war poems are so strongly marked that it is hardly surprising that critics over seventy years have described them in broadly similar terms. What seems to have happened is not that description and even evaluation have changed in this period, but that essentialist views of poetry have become less evident and less assured. For Massingham epigrams are not poems: Bergonzi is concerned only to mark Sassoon's limits *within* poetry.

Donald Davie suggests that Wilfred Owen asks to be seen as 'the English soldier of 1918', as over against Brooke, 'the English soldier of 1914'. To a considerble extent what has happened is that Owen has replaced Brooke as 'the English soldier of the First World War'. As early as 1920 Edmund Blunden spoke of Owen as 'one of the few spokesmen of the ordinary fighting man' – 'the fighting man of resolution and ability who loathed the war in theory and practice'. He is 'a poet of rare force', associated with rebellion: 'there could scarcely have been one mind in a thousand that did not rebel' (though Blunden is speaking of a rebellion of spirit rather than action). Dylan Thomas reacts similarly, although in another idiom: Owen 'is the common touch . . . He writes love-letters home for the illiterate dead. Ignorant, uncaring, hapless as the rest of the bloody troops, he is their agent shell-shocked into diction.' And John Johnston (1964) sees Owen as revolutionary in the rather vague sense that 'his work embodies, more dramatically than that of any other poet, the changing values of the time'.

There is little critical doubt that Owen is a 'true poet'. Middleton Murry, who worried about Sassoon, is confident about Owen, 'the only poet of the war'. Owen is this because he, and only he, meets Murry's criteria: 'Owen's poetry is unique and terrible because it records imperishably the devastation and the victory of a soul.' For Murry there must be resurrection after crucifixion. C. Day Lewis sees Owen as 'a true revolutionary poet, opening up new fields of sensitiveness for his successors. If he had lived there is no knowing what his promise might have achieved.' John Bayley, commenting on Owen as celebrating 'with majestic understanding that enlargement of the human spirit with makes . . . even out of war a value, like the value of love', invokes Tolstoy and Shakespeare.

When Murry offers Owen as 'the only poet of the war' we can see the displacement of Brooke, and the extended commentaries on Owen's poetry by, say, Welland and Bergonzi act as a kind of confirmation:[10] the poetry has the texture to respond to developed practical criticism; it belongs to the 'great tradition' and needs none of the special pleading used at times for Sassoon.

But there have been, and are dissenting voices. There is the attitude of Henry Newbolt in 1924, who sees Owen as one of 'the broken men' and – breathtakingly – finds that these 'haven't the experience or the imagination to know the extreme human agony', seeing in Douglas Haig 'what is truly great – perfect acceptance, which means perfect faith'. This remark, on reflection, may be a terrible, ironic truth, but Newbolt's position is absurd and offensive. More important is Yeats's famous comment that Owen is 'all blood,

dirt & sucked sugar stick'. The force of the indictment lies less in the
first two epithets (for a poetry of war without blood and dirt should
arouse suspicions of the triumph of Brooke) than in the combined
suggestion that blood and dirt in Owen's poetry are composite parts
of 'sucked sugar stick'. Lurking in Yeats's phrase is disgust: the
poetry is dirty in more than the obvious sense and the dirt
(obscenity) has suggestions of homo-eroticism as fellatio. Johnston
picks up the remark but reads it with a different stress, to define a
problem/limitation. In Owen's 'Poetry – the "sucked sugar stick"
element – was prominent, although he was gradually eliminating it
or making it the source of ironic reference.' Donald Davie picks up
another of Yeats's points and rebukes Yeats for being 'simple-
minded here', only to use the gravamen of the charge: 'Owen *does*
write badly, he is just not skilful nor resourceful enough to do justice
to his own conceptions.' More recently, John Lucas has expresssed
similar views.[11]

Since shortly after his death, Owen has been highly valued, first
by a minority of critics and fellow-poets. Since the Second World
War he has been consistently seen, by the majority of those who
know anything about the poetry of the First World War, as its finest
voice. It may seem, however, that a desire to have a great voice – the
voice of a combatant recording 'the devastation and the victory' in
appropriately bardic terms – has encouraged neglect of the problems
that troubled Davie, and Yeats before him.

In a general sense, the idea that the war produced a renaissance of
poetry may have roots in the desire to see it as good (or, at least, as
doing good), and it may also have a democratic tinge, in so far as it
promotes the idea of a poetry produced by a large number of
amateurs. Yet this line of thought crosses another, that the war ought
to produce a great poet, a bard to articulate, in epic terms, the voice
and will of the nation. The reception of poetry of the First World
War suggests that this role was first filled by Brooke and later by
Owen, while something along these lines may also be seen in some
criticism of Rosenberg, with, for instance, Sassoon's emphasis on the
epithets 'Scriptural and sculptural' as appropriate to Rosenberg's
verse, or in Silkin's desire to have a Rosenberg who enunciates
general truths about the war. (Sassoon, by this kind of account,
would be the voice of counterpoint, of the anti-heroic as against the
heroic.)

A dialogue between the 'democratic' and 'bardic' emphases can be seen reflected in, on the one hand, anthologies which present a large number of poets (Osborn, Hibberd/Onions) and, on the other, works of criticism which focus on a small number of the 'best' authors (Enright, Silkin). This comparison suggests also a division in valuing, between those who emphasise the significance of material regardless of quality and those who, by rigorous selection, intimate that the aesthetically most satisfying poets are the most significant voices of the war.

If Poetry is an absolute, it should be possible (theoretically) to work out which poems of the war (if any) attain absolute excellence; and the concept of the absolute would mean that such poems would simultaneously be the most significant accounts of the war, since they would be the ones which relate experience of the war to eternal truths. But if it is argued that the First World War is, above all else, a phenomenon of our century, a vital aspect of this part of history, it can be claimed that transcendent poetry is not what should be most valued, and that a materialist account is essential. It might, however, be alleged that the poles are not antithetical, but can cohabit. According to this argument, the greatest poetry is that which combines consideration of major human experience with technique fully expressive of that experience. Such an argument begs some big theoretical questions, but it is enough here to make two points. First, it does not deal with the issue of what aspects of experience are 'major', or for whom, or of what perspectives are appropriate for the treatment of the selected aspects. To a wealthy aristocrat food may be important largely as a symbol of wealth; to a peasant it is likely to be a desperately concrete need. If Yeats is right to suggest that 'joy' is fundamental to tragedy, and if 'tragedy' is a 'major' human issue, *King Lear* is not tragic and *Hamlet* is a satire on tragedy. Second, the formula can scarcely work for the First World War, because the verse which is, in terms of the formula, the most successful, concerns itself almost entirely with limited though highly important, aspects of war experience. The account provided by this verse would have it that the response of non-enthusiastic combatants is *the* significant truth of the war. Home responses, women's responses, enthusiast responses – all become marginal. And although some might argue that this is a proper hierarchy, it seems to me to exclude too much, and in doing so to misrepresent a war that was so complex and so profound in its effects as to call for/enforce variety of response – and a questioning of the whole idea of absolute truth. It is no simple accident that the First World War asks to be seen as an aspect of Modernism, the roots of which are deeply suspicious of essential verities.

Although the issue of how to value the verse of and about the First World War is far from easy, my own view is simply enough stated. It is that there is a point where, for human beings, art is less important than life. Arguments that the former enriches and interprets the latter are beside the point in its full nakedness, which says that the *fact* of an infant's body in the terminal stages of dysentery in Bangladesh or of starvation in the Sudan is more important than – more *fundamental* than – a Beethoven symphony or a Van Gogh painting. Another way of saying this would be to state that such recognition of such awful facts must underlie any worthwhile view of art. And it follows that perception of life's fundamentals is more important than art can be, and that art's most important function is to assist such perception (and to help perceivers find ways of avoiding despair). If the First World War is thus more important than poetry (a more important fact in our experience than any artefact or even all artefacts) we can make sense of some remarks of Donald Davie's. He is discussing Yeats's famous rejection of Owen (as developed and endorsed by Johnston – see above). Speaking of Owen's 'Greater Love' and Rosenberg's 'Dead Man's Dump', he asks 'If we are moved when we read them, far more moved (this is certainly my own case) than by Yeats's 'Irish Airman', ought we to be ashamed?' He goes on to suggest that 'Certainly as a poem in any strict sense "Dead Man's Dump" is indefensible', adding 'But the truth is surely that for the British reader these pieces by Rosenberg and Owen are not poems at all, but something less than that and more; they are first-hand and faithful witnesses to a moment in the national destiny'.[12] This is, I think, laboured and rather evasive ('something less than that and more'), but it does admit the primacy of life; whereby Owen's inefficiency with rhyme is transcended.

Taken together, two of Owen's poems may clarify the point. 'Futility' seems to me one of Owen's most fully achieved poems – deeply moving, technically satisfying, and impressively forcing a reader to make connections between the war and the vast issue of the origins and (possible) purpose of human life. By contrast, the sestet of 'Anthem for Doomed Youth' – after an octet of distinction comparable with 'Futility' – is a disappointing and sentimental shimmer of Brookean melancholy; the game being betrayed by line 12's bad pun – 'The pallor of girl's brows shall be their pall'. But the badness is revealing and thus instructive. As late as September 1917 as intelligent a man as Owen, and even with the help of Sassoon, found it difficult to fight off the impulse to indulge feeling at the expense of thought. If we simply say that the sestet is bad, and value 'Futility' above 'Anthem . . .' because it lacks such badness, we are in danger of missing what the sestet can show.

What it shows, I think, is the importance of 'cultural materialism'. If, instead of operating in a New Critical vacuum, we see the 'bad' sestet as a product of a particular time and situation, we can value it as a revealing moment in the history of the war. Along the same lines, it is possible to argue that Brooke's sonnet 'The Soldier' is quite an adroit and moving statement of its chauvinistic theme, while taking the view that it is only a 'good' poem on purely formal grounds and suggesting that its value (like the value of Churchill's eulogy of Brooke) lies in its unwitting revelation of attitudes conducive to wars. Brooke's art here, I would argue, should finally be validated by revealing its inadequate base and obliterating itself with the revelation.

So long as we accept that understanding as much as possible about the First World War is very important for our own lives and possible futures, and that the greatest urgency is to see how repetition can be prevented (but the pictures from the Iraq/Iran fronts looked much like the Somme), we should be able to see that a number of critical viewpoints about the war's poetry must be resisted or redefined. The position of Edward Thomas is a case in point. Robert Frost wrote that Thomas did not think of his own poetry as war poetry, 'though that is what it is'.[13] Getting this accepted is not primarily a matter of literary classification, but of ensuring that Thomas's particular response to the war is always a part of the record, and specifically of the struggle against the false patriotism which facilitates war. There is also the complex issue of Ivor Gurney. The particular merits of Gurney's verse are very important and call for sustained critical analysis. But it is also important to locate his product. It has been observed, accurately enough, that Gurney's asylum poems (and letters) fluctuate between 'madness' and 'sanity'. Even without questioning these terms it is important to grasp what such product signifies: the part the war played in the destruction of a human being and, more generally, the part played by a culture which produced the war and could not save Gurney. We might also remember that he was not the only participant in the war who spent time in asylums. To seek to confine Gurney to aesthetics is itself a form of madness.

More generally, it follows that to exclude the bulk of the war's verse because it is untalented or says the 'wrong' things is a mistake. Where such exclusion is justified on grounds of quality, we should remember that the war is more important than art. More positively, we should consider what it signifies that Owen cannot write colloquially or MacGill find a voice to match his background and experience. MacGill's poems should be known *because* they testify to the missing voice and because they articulate the pressures on the mass to emulate the voices and values of their class superiors. Similarly, poems by officers which fail to find a convincing voice for the ranker are important in their failure, helping us to qualify those moving assertions of oneness with 'their' ranker 'boys'. The poems which reduce Britain to Eton or New College or a Berkshire village need to be known because that complacency is instructive and part of the record; while the poems of chivalric history are similarly significant. Poetry of the war by women should need no apology, nor should its 'revival' be open to question. The voices of over half the population must be attended to, being a part of the record.

This may seem to be levelling, even reductivist, and to deny any merit to the long-respectable pursuit of valuing and the techniques developed in that cause. It certainly does not, in my view, devalue analytic techniques – though it may utilise them to different ends. It does seek to open up the issue of valuing, so that incoherence and conventionality, for instance, may be seen to have value for us in the pursuit of understanding (as verbal slips may do, or mixed metaphors). And it does call into question the authority of the single author, even of the autonomous individual. But if understanding remains our objective, and if to understand is to relate as many elements of experience as possible in coherent form, it follows that valuing continues to have its place. Gurney, to me, understands more – and in understanding coordinates more – than Brooke. Should I then ignore the fact that Gurney had more cause to understand more, what this signifies, what Brooke understood and misunderstood? Moreover, if we are not dealing with absolutes (and I do not see how we can be) we can only deal as openly and as honestly as possible with valuings rather than with value.

## NOTES

1. Modern Humanities Research Association.
2. See page 83f.
3. Nicholson and Watson, 1943.
4. *Out of Battle*, Oxford, 1972.
5. Weidenfeld and Nicolson, 1969.
6. *The Pelican Guide to English Literature: The modern age*, Penguin, 1961.
7. Batsford, 1986.
8. See, for instance, the index to Liddell Hart.
9. *Poetry of the First World War*, Macmillan, 1981. References for the remainder of this chapter are from this collection unless otherwise stated.
10. *Wilfred Owen*, Chatto and Windus, 1960; *Heroes' Twilight*, Constable, 1965.
11. See note 7, above.
12. Davie, in Hibberd, p. 110.
13. Quoted by William Cooke, in Hibberd, p. 238.

# CONCLUSION

I have been reading J.M. Bourne's excellent *Britain and the Great War 1914–1918* (Arnold, 1989). It is to some extent revisionist, arguing, for instance, that the Battle of the Somme achieved the objectives set by Haig and that these were important objectives for the outcome of the war. Bourne's book also makes the case for Admiral Jellicoe, who has had a poor press. Bourne writes to provide a reassessment of aspects of the history of the war, knowing that this involves him in debate with other historians and in a struggle with myths.

There can be few conclusions about the First World War which stand or will stand as conclusive; and that is itself a grim tribute to the importance of the war in our century (an importance recently marked in Ted Hughes's volume *Wolfwatching*). If so, there can be few conclusive conclusions about the poetry of the war. By itself poetry does not make war or bring a war to an end or prevent another war. But if poetry can and does have an active social role it may contribute to the presence or absence of war. If war is always an evil, to be avoided wherever possible, and if poetry does have an active social role, it follows that poems which endorse or encourage war are dangerous (however good the poems may aesthetically be) – as is criticism which endorses such poetry. Conversely, poetry which works to obstruct war is healthy. The task of the poetry, as of the criticism which attends it, is to maximise the obstruction, although this is not some simple issue of slogans and banners. The fact that neither the questioning poems of the war nor criticism of the war's poetry has outlawed war in the decades since 1918 is saddening, but no excuse for abandoning the effort by seeking for 'pure' poetry and so-called dispassionate criticism.

The finest poems of the war obstruct war by encouraging serious thought and feeling, and the critic's business is to encourage recognition of this. Her/his business is also, however, to try to understand and communicate what happens with poetry that does not obstruct: to reveal it for what it, dangerously, is. The objective of poetry about war, as of the associated criticism, should be to deconstruct itself by removing the occasion of its very existence.

# REFERENCES

References here are to original dates of publication. In the text, however, different editions are sometimes used, as indicated in the notes.

## INDIVIDUAL VOLUMES OF POEMS

Aldington, R., *Collected Poems*, Allen and Unwin, 1929.
Arkwright, J., *The Supreme Sacrifice*, Skeffington, 1919.
Binyon, L., *The Winnowing Fan*, Elkin Mathews, 1914.
Brooke, R., *The Poems*, ed. T. Rogers, Black Swan, 1987.
Brooke, R., *The Collected Poems, with a Memoir by Edward Marsh*, Sidgwick and Jackson, 1918.
Clark, T.B., *Poems of a Private*, Nicholson, n.d.
Dobell, B., *Songs and Lyrics of the War*, Dobell, 1915.
Gibson, W.W., *Battle*, Elkin Mathews, 1915.
Graves, R., *Poems About War*, ed. W. Graves, Cassell, 1988.
Gurney, I., *Severn and Somme/War's Embers*, ed. R.K. Thornton, MidNag/Carcanet, 1987.
Gurney, I., *Collected Poems*, ed. P.J. Kavanagh, Oxford, 1982.
Harvey, F., *Gloucestershire Friends*, Sidgwick and Jackson, 1917.
Kennedy, G. Studdert, *The Unutterable Beauty*, Hodder and Stoughton, n.d.
Lee, J., *Ballads of Battle*, Murray, 1916.
Lee, J., *Work-a-Day Warriors*, Murray, 1917.
MacGill, P., *Soldier Songs*, Jenkins, 1917.
Newbolt, H., *Poems Old and New*, Murray, 1919.
Newbolt, H., *Collected Poems*, Nelson, n.d.
Nichols, R., *Ardours and Endurances*, Chatto and Windus, 1918.
Owen, W., *Collected Poems*, ed. E. Blunden, Chatto and Windus, 1963.
Owen, W., *War Poems and Others*, ed. D. Hibberd, Chatto and Windus, 1973.

Read, H., *Collected Poems,* Faber, 1956.

Rosenberg, I., *Collected Poems,* ed. G. Bottomley and D. Harding, Chatto and Windus, 1937.

Sassoon, S., *The War Poems,* Faber, 1983.

Sorley, C., *The Poems and Selected Letters,* ed. H.D. Spear, Blackness Press, 1978.

Thomas, E., *The Collected Poems,* ed. R. George Thomas, Oxford, 1981.

Watson, W., *Collected Poems,* John Lane, 1898.

## ANTHOLOGIES OF POEMS

Black, E. (ed.), *1914–18 in Poetry,* Hodder and Stoughton, 1970.

Clarke, G.H. (ed.), *A Treasury of War Poetry,* Houghton Mifflin, 1917.

Gardner, B. (ed.), *Up the Line to Death,* Methuen, 1964.

Hibberd, D. and Onions, J. (eds.), *Poetry of the Grear War,* Macmillan, 1986.

Hussey, M. (ed.), *Poetry of the First World War,* Longman, 1976.

*More Songs by the Fighting Men,* Erskine MacDonald, 1917.

Nichols, R. (ed.), *Anthology of War Poetry 1914–1918,* Nicholson and Watson, 1943.

Osborn, E.B. (ed.), *The Muse in Arms,* Murray, 1918.

Parsons, I. (ed.), *Men who March Away,* Chatto and Windus, 1965.

Reilly, C. (ed.), *Scars upon my Heart,* Virago, 1981.

Silkin, J. (ed.), *The Penguin Book of First World War Poetry,* Penguin, 1979.

*Soldier Poets: Songs of the fighting men,* Erskine MacDonald, 1916.

Trotter, J. (ed.), *Valour and Vision,* Hopkinson, 1920.

Tulloch, D. (ed.), *Songs and Poems of the Great World War,* Davis Press, 1915.

## OTHER PRIMARY TEXTS

Bairsnfather, B., *The Best of Fragments from France,* ed. T. and V. Holt, Milestone, 1978.

Blunden, E., *Undertones of War,* Penguin, 1928.

Coppard, G., *With a Machine Gun from Cambrai,* HMSO, 1969.

Graves, R., *Goodbye to All That,* Cassell, 1929.

Laffin, J. (ed.), *Letters from the Front,* Dent, 1975.

Sassoon, S., *Memoirs of a Fox-hunting Man,* Faber, 1928.

Wood, J. (ed.), *A Life Well Lived: A memoir of J.W.C. Taylor,* Partridge, n.d.


## SECONDARY SOURCES


Adcock, A. St J., *For Remembrance,* Hodder and Stoughton, n.d.

Allison, W. and Fairley, J., *The Monocled Mutineer,* Quartet, 1979.

Babington, A., *For the Sake of Example,* Leo Cooper, 1983.

Cohn, N., *The Pursuit of the Millennium,* Secker and Warburg, 1957.

Delany, P., *The Neo-Pagans,* Macmillan, 1987.

Ford, B. (ed.), *The Pelican Guide to English Literature: The modern age,* Penguin, 1961.

Fussell, P., *The Great War and Modern Memory,* Oxford, 1975.

Gay, P., *Weimar Culture,* Secker and Warburg, 1969.

Hamburger, M., *The Truth of Poetry,* Weidenfeld and Nicolson, 1969.

Hammerton, J.A. (ed.), *War Illustrated,* Amalgamated Press, n.d.

Hart, B. Liddell, *History of the First World War,* Cassell, 1934.

Haste, C., *Keep the Home Fires Burning,* Allen Lane, 1977.

Hibberd, D. (ed.), *Poetry of the First World War,* Macmillan, 1981.

Hobsbawm, E., *The Age of Empire,* Book Club Associates, 1987.

Hoehling, A.A., *The Great War at Sea,* Barker, n.d.

Howarth, P., *Play Up and Play the Game,* Eyre Methuen, 1973.

Keen, M., *Chivalry,* Yale University Press, 1984.

Khan, N., *Women's Poetry of the First World War,* Harvester Wheatsheaf, 1988.

Lawson, J. and Silver, H., *A Social History of Education in England,* Methuen, 1973.

Lucas, J., *Modern English Poetry – from Hardy to Hughes,* Batsford, 1986.

Osborn, E.B., *The New Elizabethans,* John Lane, 1919.

Read, D., *England 1865-1914,* Longman, 1979.

Read, J.M., *Atrocity Propaganda,* Yale University Press, 1941.

Silkin, J., *Out of Battle,* Oxford, 1972.

Steiner, Z., *Britain and the Origins of the First World War,* Macmillan, 1977.

Taylor, A.J.P., *The First World War: An illustrated history,* Hamish Hamilton, 1963.

Terraine, J., *The Smoke and the Fire,* Sidgwick & Jackson, 1980.

Thompson, P., *The Edwardians,* Weidenfeld and Nicolson, 1975.

Tuchman, B., *The Proud Tower,* Macmillan, 1962.

Wohl, R., *The Generation of 1914,* Weidenfeld and Nicolson, 1980.

# INDEX